Mathematics for Christian Living Series

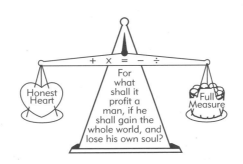

Mathematics for Christian Living Series

Working Arithmetic

Grade 2

Unit 3, Lessons 61–102

Rod and Staff Publishers, Inc.

P.O. Box 3, Hwy. 172

Crockett, Kentucky 41413

Telephone: (606) 522-4348

Acknowledgments

We are indebted to God for the vision of the need for a *Mathematics for Christian Living Series* and for His enabling grace. Charitable contributions from many churches have helped to cover the expenses for research and development.

This revision was written by Sisters Miriam Rudolph and Marla Martin. The brethren Marvin Eicher, Jerry Kreider, and Luke Sensenig served as editors. Most of the illustrations were drawn by Lois Myer. The work was evaluated by a panel of reviewers and tested by teachers in the classroom. Much effort was devoted to the production of the book. We are grateful for all who helped to make this book possible.

—The Publishers

This book is part of a course for grade 2 arithmetic and will be most effective if used with the other parts of the course. *Working Arithmetic* includes the following items:

Teacher's Manual, part 1 (Units 1, 2)
Teacher's Manual, part 2 (Units 3–5)
Pupil's Workbook, Unit 1
Pupil's Workbook, Unit 2
Pupil's Workbook, Unit 3
Pupil's Workbook, Unit 4
Pupil's Workbook, Unit 5
Blacklines

16   17   —   22   21   20   19

Unit 3 Contents

This list shows what concepts are introduced in these lessons. Each concept is also reviewed in following lessons.

61. (12) 9 3 triplet and facts
    2 digits + 2 digits + 1 digit
62.
63.
64. Place value: 1's, 10's, 100's, 1,000's
65.
66. (12) 8 4 triplet and facts
67. Carrying: 2 digits + 2 digits
68.
69.
70.
71. (12) 7 5 triplet and facts
72
73.
74. Clocks—:15
75.
76. (12) 6 6 triplet and facts
77.
78. Reading Problem: Key word—*both*
79. (13) 9 4 triplet and facts
80.
81. Clocks—:45
82.

83.
84. Column addition—carrying
    Shapes: circle, square
85. Shape: triangle
86.
87. Shape: rectangle
88.
89.
90. Borrowing: 2 digits − 2 digits
91.
92.
93.
94.
95. (13) 7 6 triplet and facts
96.
97.
98. $ sign and decimal point
99.
100. Fraction: $\frac{1}{2}$
     Reading Problem: missing part
101.
102.

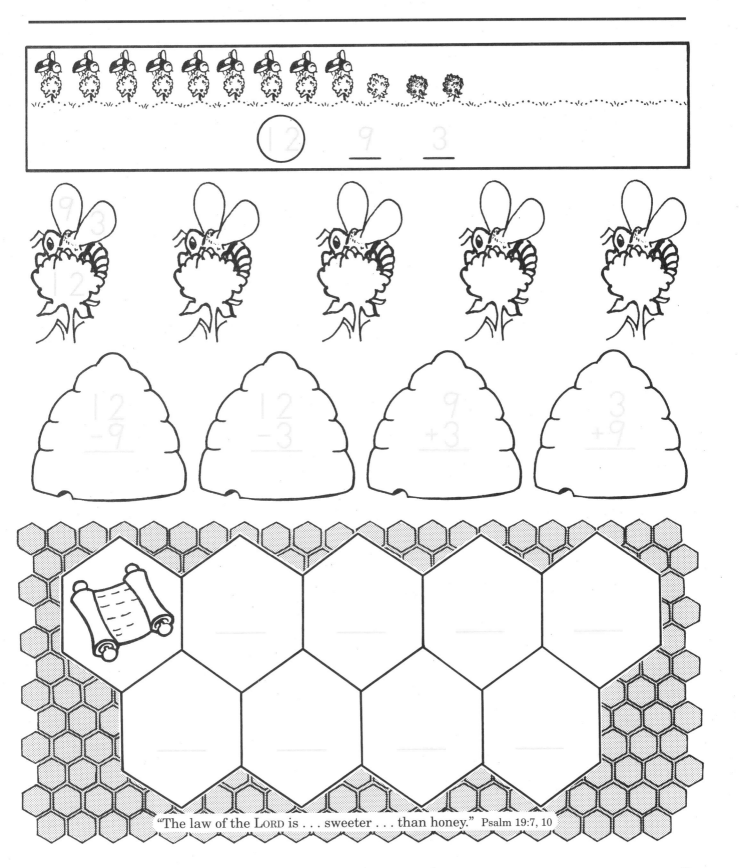

"The law of the LORD is . . . sweeter . . . than honey." Psalm 19:7, 10

9 +3	12 −9	12 −3	3 +9	12 −9	9 +3	12 −9	12 −3
12 −3	3 +9	12 −9	9 +3	12 −3	3 +9	9 +3	12 −9
12 −3	12 −9	3 +9	12 −9	9 +3	12 −3	12 −9	3 +9
12 −9	9 +3	12 −3	3 +9	12 −9	12 −3	9 +3	12 −9
12 −9	12 −3	12 −9	12 −3	12 −9	9 +3	3 +9	12 −9
		12 −9	3 +9	12 −3	12 −9	9 +3	12 −3

```
  32      33      33      64      74      22
  53      22      21      32      21      14
 +24     +62     +65     +33     +32     +93
_____  _____  _____  _____  _____  _____
```

```
  14      44      55      23      35      42
  53      31      32      72      60      55
 + 2     + 2     + 2     + 4     + 2     + 2
_____  _____  _____  _____  _____  _____
```

"His eye
seeth every
precious thing."

Job 28:10

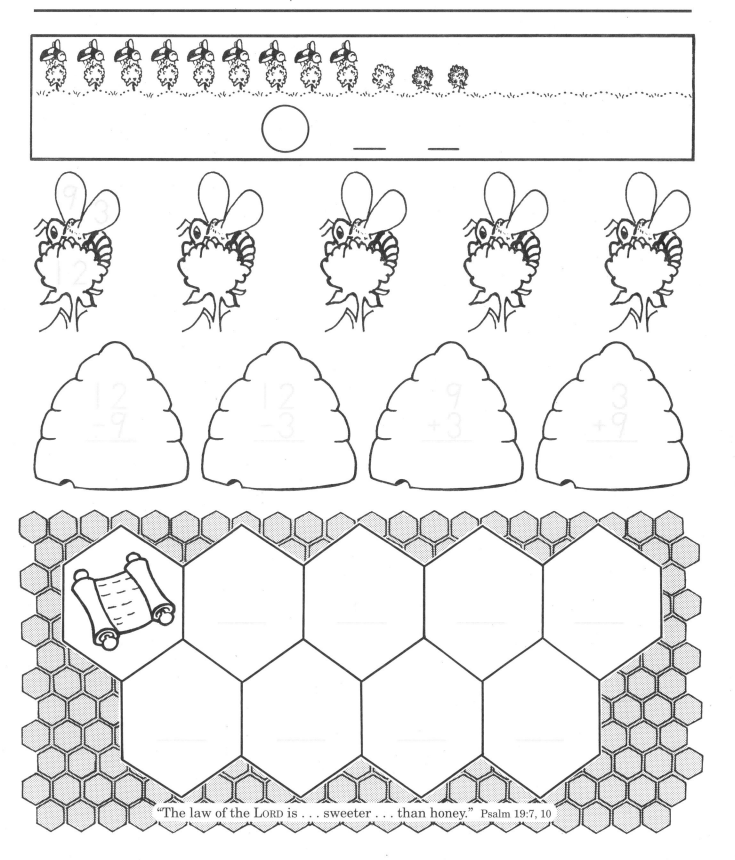

"The law of the LORD is . . . sweeter . . . than honey." Psalm 19:7, 10

```
 124      93      126      125       36      128
 -93     +32      -34      -91      +92      -36
_____    _____    _____    _____    _____    _____


  96     129       32      127       93      127
 +33     -98      +95      -34      +35      -92
_____    _____    _____    _____    _____    _____


  34     128      127      127      129       94
 +91     -97      -93      -35      -37      +34
_____    _____    _____    _____    _____    _____


 127      97      128       34      129       91
 -96     +32      -35      +93      -94      +37
_____    _____    _____    _____    _____    _____


 129      32      128       93       32      128
 -35     +93      -92      +31      +90      -33
_____    _____    _____    _____    _____    _____
```

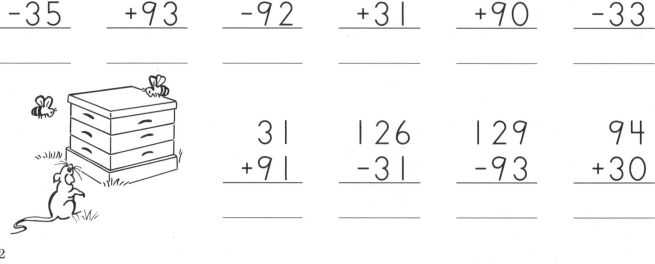

```
          31      126      129       94
         +91      -31      -93      +30
        _____    _____    _____    _____
```

62

 956   192   86   763   60   8

 815   59   892   6   802   30

 904   132   87   769   465   58

_____   _____   _____   _____   _____

_____   _____   _____   _____   _____

_____   _____   _____   _____   _____

13

Speed
Drill

3	12	9	12	9	12
+9	-3	+3	-9	+3	-3

9	3	12	3	12	12
+3	+9	-9	+9	-3	-9

3	12	12	3	12	9	12	9
+9	-9	-3	+9	-9	+3	-3	+3

12	9	12	12	3	12	9	3
-9	+3	-9	-3	+9	-9	+3	+9

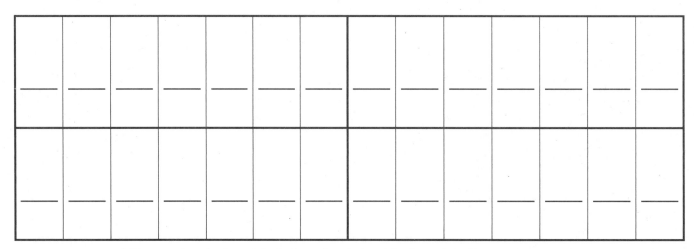

"Whatsoever thy hand findeth to do, do it with thy might." Ecclesiastes 9:10

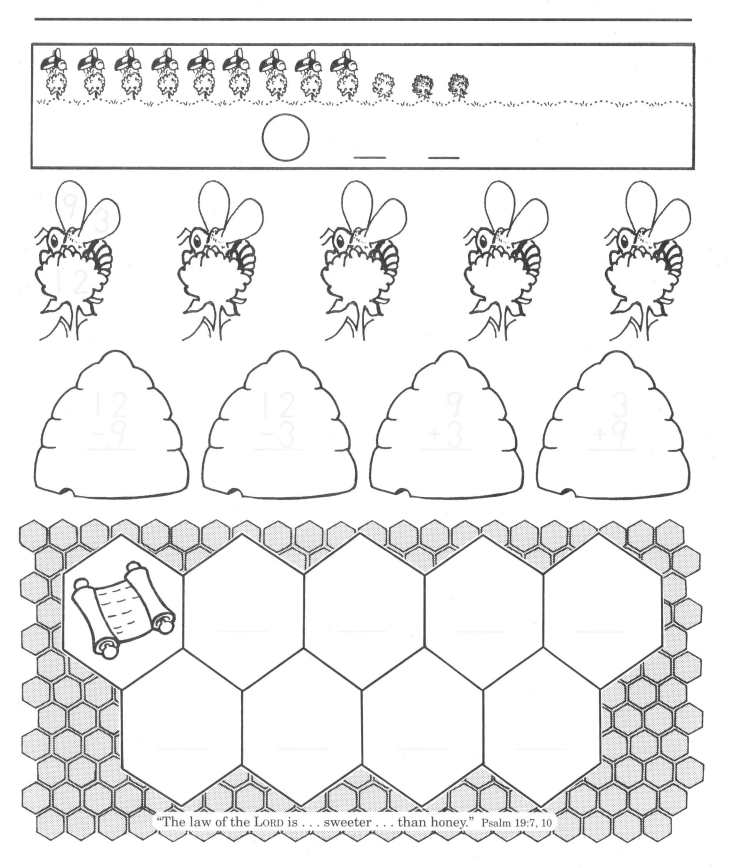

"The law of the LORD is . . . sweeter . . . than honey."   Psalm 19:7, 10

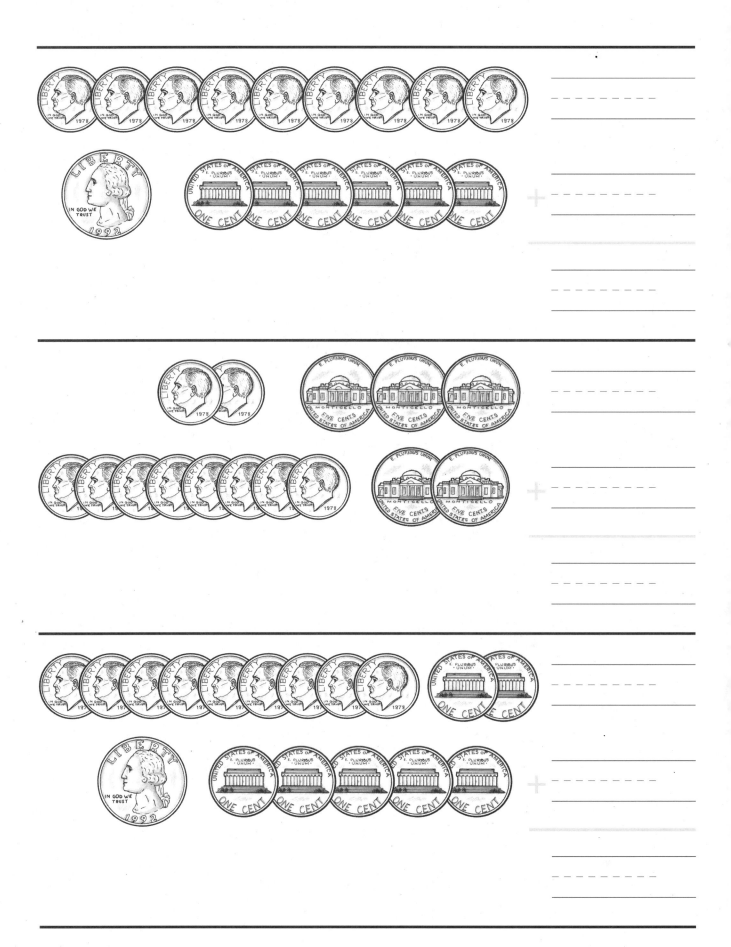

9 +3	11 −6	12 −3	6 +5	12 −9	9 +3	11 −6	11 −5

12 −3	5 +6	12 −9	6 +5	12 −3	3 +9	9 +3	12 −9

11 −5	11 −6	3 +9	12 −9	5 +6	12 −3	11 −6	3 +9

"His eye
seeth every
precious thing."

Job 28:10

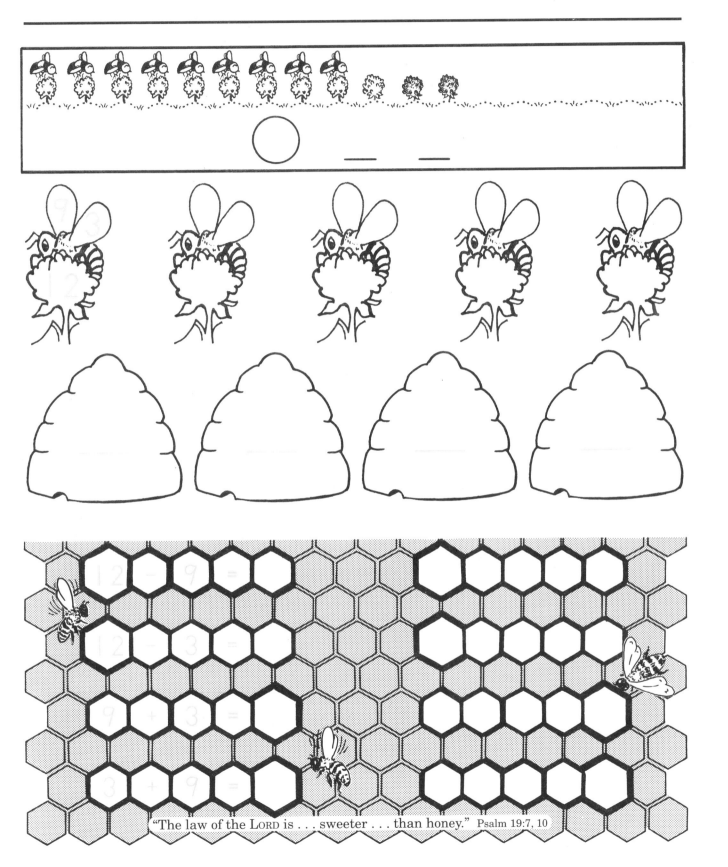

"The law of the LORD is . . . sweeter . . . than honey." Psalm 19:7, 10

$9 + \underline{} = 12$	$12 - \underline{} = 3$	$\underline{} - 3 = 9$
$3 + \underline{} = 12$	$\underline{} + 9 = 12$	$3 + \underline{} = 12$
$12 - \underline{} = 3$	$\underline{} - 9 = 3$	$12 - 9 = \underline{}$
$12 - \underline{} = 9$	$12 - 3 = \underline{}$	$\underline{} - 3 = 9$
$\underline{} + 9 = 12$	$3 + \underline{} = 12$	$3 + \underline{} = 12$
$\underline{} - 9 = 3$	$9 + 3 = \underline{}$	$\underline{} - 9 = 3$

$$
\begin{array}{cccccccc}
6 & 3 & 1 & 4 & 8 & 3 & 7 & 1 \\
3 & 2 & 2 & 5 & 1 & 6 & 2 & 1 \\
+3 & +5 & +9 & +2 & +3 & +3 & +3 & +9 \\
\hline
\end{array}
$$

$$
\begin{array}{cccccccc}
5 & 9 & 2 & 4 & 5 & 1 & 1 & 2 \\
4 & 0 & 7 & 5 & 3 & 8 & 6 & 1 \\
+2 & +3 & +3 & +3 & +3 & +3 & +3 & +9 \\
\hline
\end{array}
$$

	thousands	hundreds	tens	ones
1583	___,	___	___	___
1815	___,	___	___	___
80	___,	___	___	___
293	___,	___	___	___
1325	___,	___	___	___
1784	___,	___	___	___
1623	___,	___	___	___

	thousands	hundreds	tens	ones
1639	___,	___	___	___
1298	___,	___	___	___
20	___,	___	___	___
1315	___,	___	___	___
290	___,	___	___	___
1324	___,	___	___	___
1816	___,	___	___	___

_____ _____ _____ _____ _____

_____ _____ _____ _____ _____

_____ _____ _____ _____ _____

_____ _____ _____ _____ _____

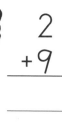

Speed Drill

3 +9	12 −3	11 −2	9 +2	11 −9	12 −9

2 +9	12 −3	9 +3	12 −9	9 +2	3 +9

12 −3	3 +9	12 −9	11 −9	2 +9	12 −3	11 −2	9 +3

3 +9	12 −3	9 +3	2 +9	12 −9	3 +9	11 −2	9 +2

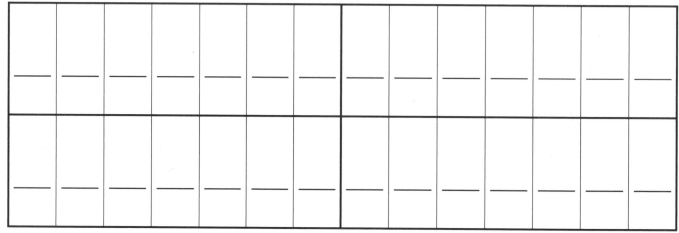

"Whatsoever thy hand findeth to do, do it with thy might." Ecclesiastes 9:10

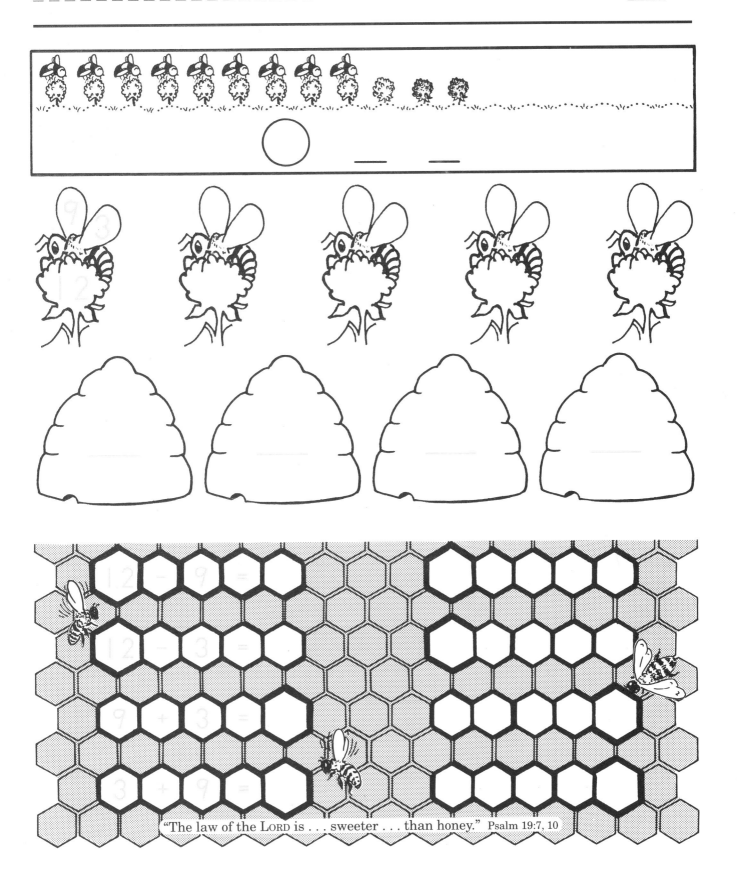

"The law of the LORD is . . . sweeter . . . than honey." Psalm 19:7, 10

Jane can say nine verses from the Bible. Her little sister can say 3 verses. How many verses is that altogether?

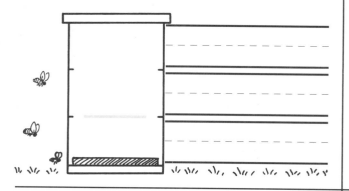

Lee saw 3 flocks of geese flying south. Fred saw 9 flocks. How many flocks was that in all?

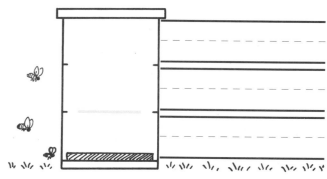

Mother has 12 quilts in a chest. She gives 3 quilts to a mother in need. How many quilts are left in the chest?

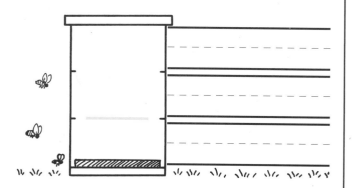

12 frogs sit on a rock. Nine of them hop into the pond. How many frogs are left on the rock?

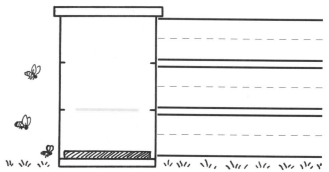

7	12	12	3	11	5	12
+4	-9	-3	+9	-7	+6	-9

11
-5

11	3	11	9	11	3	9
-4	+9	-6	+3	-4	+9	+3

11
-6

11	12	6	11	9	12	12
-5	-9	+5	-7	+3	-3	-9

4
+7

	thousands	hundreds	tens	ones
1295	____ ,	____	____	____
37	____ ,	____	____	____
1315	____ ,	____	____	____
290	____ ,	____	____	____
1324	____ ,	____	____	____
1816	____ ,	____	____	____

	thousands	hundreds	tens	ones
1815	____ ,	____	____	____
380	____ ,	____	____	____
1293	____ ,	____	____	____
1325	____ ,	____	____	____
1784	____ ,	____	____	____
1623	____ ,	____	____	____

25

"His eye
seeth every
precious thing."

Job 28:10

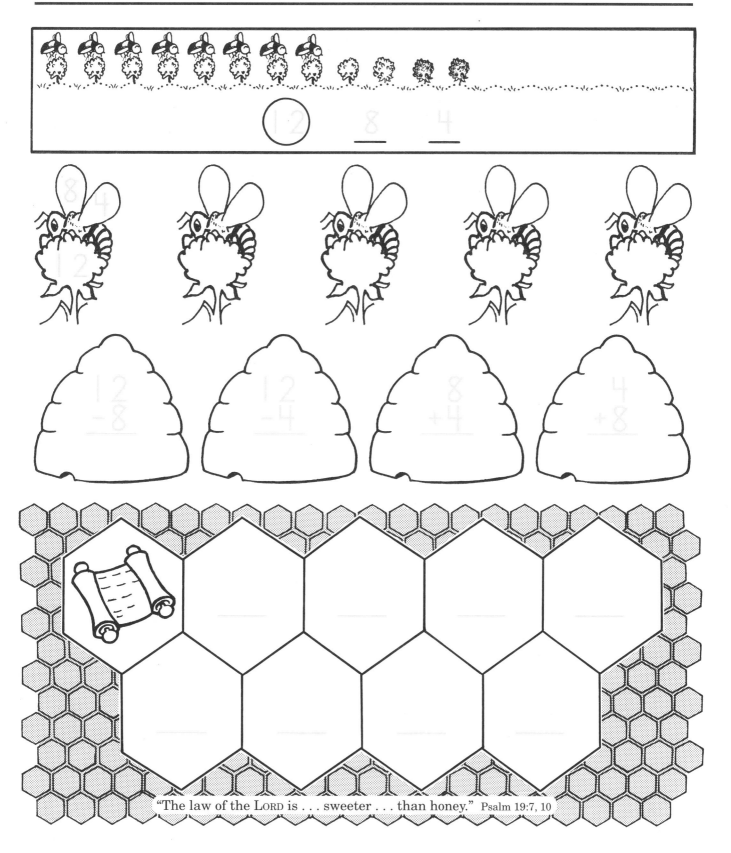

"The law of the LORD is . . . sweeter . . . than honey." Psalm 19:7, 10

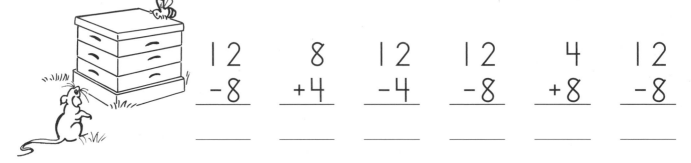

4 +8	12 −8	12 −4	8 +4	12 −8	4 +8	12 −4	12 −8

12 −4	8 +4	12 −8	4 +8	12 −4	8 +4	4 +8	12 −8

12 −8	12 −4	8 +4	12 −8	4 +8	12 −4	12 −8	8 +4

12 −4	4 +8	12 −8	8 +4	12 −8	12 −4	4 +8	12 −8

12 −8	12 −4	12 −8	12 −4	12 −8	4 +8	8 +4	12 −8

12 −8	8 +4	12 −4	12 −8	4 +8	12 −8

	thousands	hundreds	tens	ones
1948	___,	___	___	___
306	___,	___	___	___
1680	___,	___	___	___
93	___,	___	___	___
1945	___,	___	___	___
1784	___,	___	___	___
1623	___,	___	___	___

	thousands	hundreds	tens	ones
639	___,	___	___	___
1582	___,	___	___	___
607	___,	___	___	___
1315	___,	___	___	___
1290	___,	___	___	___
324	___,	___	___	___
1816	___,	___	___	___

Speed Drill

11	11	5	3	2	11
−8	−7	+6	+9	+9	−2

11	8	11	11	9	11
−5	+3	−7	−6	+3	−4

6	3	12	4	9	5	11	12
+5	+9	−3	+7	+3	+6	−7	−9

3	7	11	9	11	11	3	11
+9	+4	−4	+3	−6	−7	+8	−5

"Whatsoever thy hand findeth to do, do it with thy might." Ecclesiastes 9:10

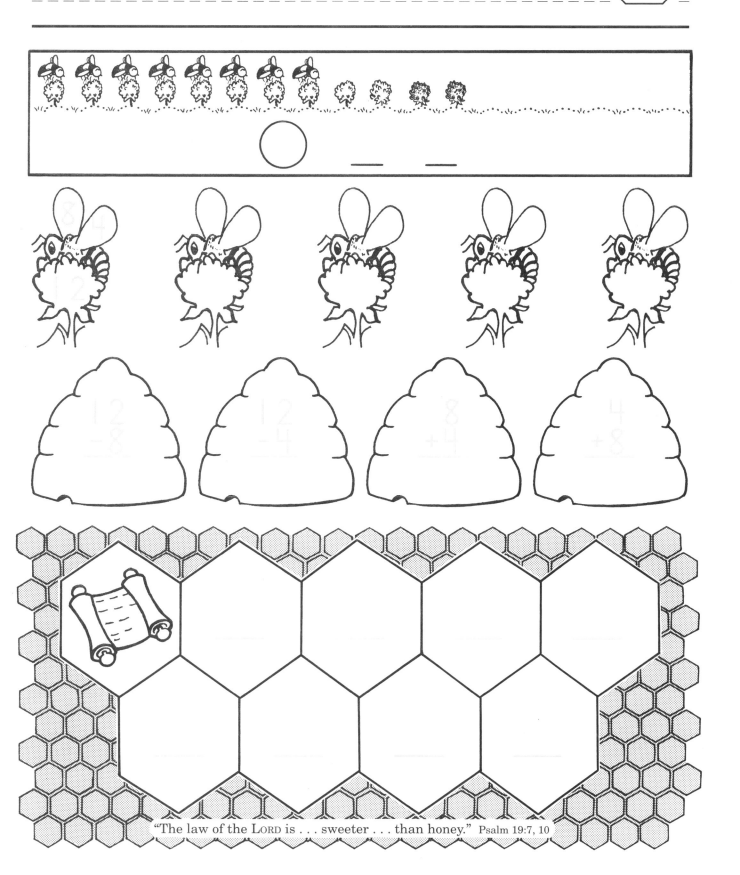

"The law of the LORD is . . . sweeter . . . than honey." Psalm 19:7, 10

31

129 -88	84 +45	129 -46	127 -83	42 +86	129 -42
83 +43	128 -83	43 +82	129 -46	85 +42	129 -83
48 +81	128 -87	128 -84	128 -45	128 -41	88 +40
129 -84	42 +84	128 -45	81 +44	128 -82	43 +84
129 -89	82 +42	128 -48	44 +83	86 +42	129 -88
		43 +85	125 -84	127 -47	82 +45

↓	↓	↓	↓	↓	↓
58	35	84	39	77	27
+44	+86	+36	+63	+43	+94

↓	↓	↓	↓	↓	↓
43	18	66	74	24	35
+69	+92	+45	+38	+87	+75

A farmer has 12 sheep in a pen. 8 sheep get out of the pen and run away. How many sheep are in the pen now?

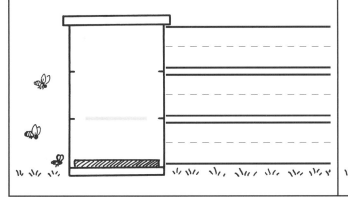

Mother fills a dish with 12 dips of ice cream. Four dips melt. How many dips are left?

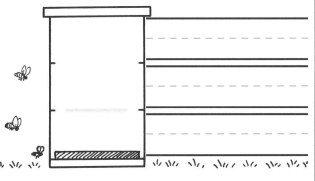

"His eye
seeth every
precious thing."

Job 28:10

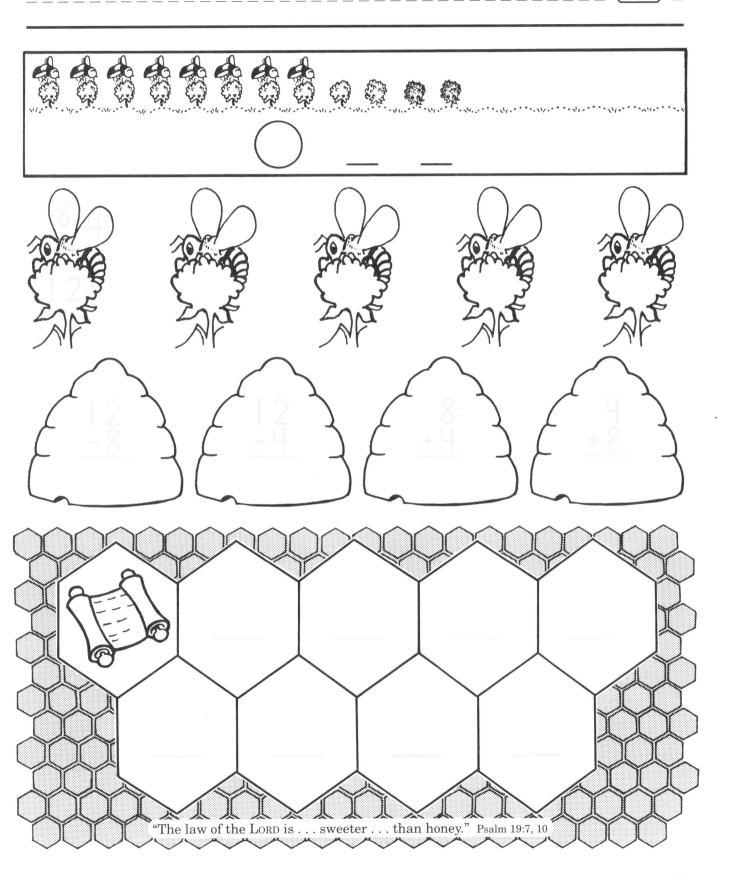

"The law of the LORD is . . . sweeter . . . than honey." Psalm 19:7, 10

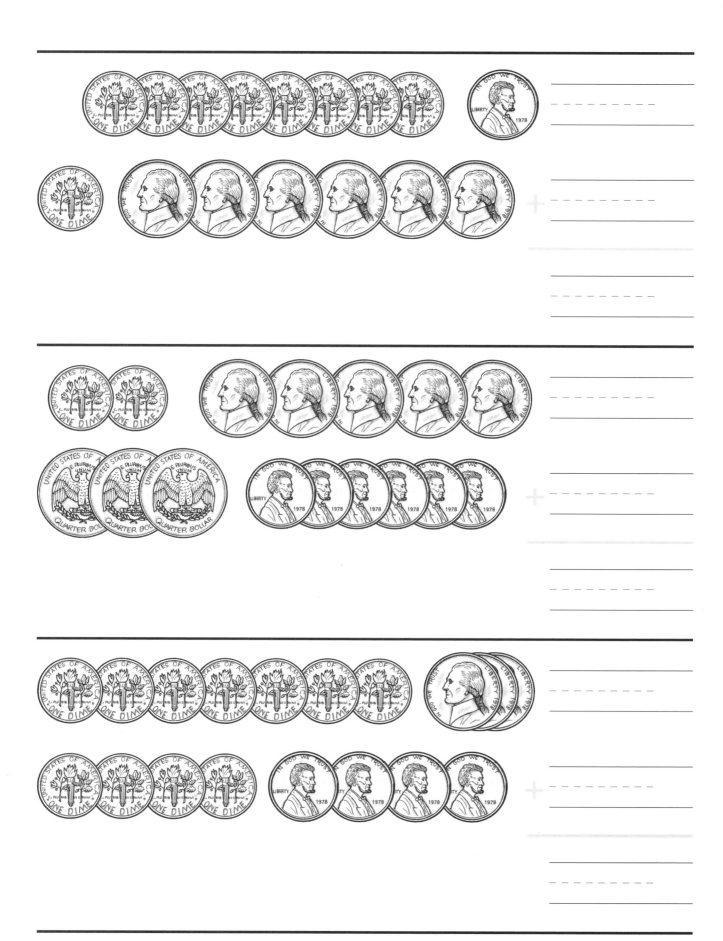

$$\begin{array}{r} \downarrow \\ 39 \\ +63 \\ \hline \end{array} \qquad \begin{array}{r} \downarrow \\ 35 \\ +86 \\ \hline \end{array} \qquad \begin{array}{r} \downarrow \\ 77 \\ +43 \\ \hline \end{array} \qquad \begin{array}{r} \downarrow \\ 43 \\ +69 \\ \hline \end{array} \qquad \begin{array}{r} \downarrow \\ 35 \\ +75 \\ \hline \end{array} \qquad \begin{array}{r} \downarrow \\ 66 \\ +45 \\ \hline \end{array}$$

$$\begin{array}{r} \downarrow \\ 18 \\ +92 \\ \hline \end{array} \qquad \begin{array}{r} \downarrow \\ 74 \\ +38 \\ \hline \end{array} \qquad \begin{array}{r} \downarrow \\ 84 \\ +36 \\ \hline \end{array} \qquad \begin{array}{r} \downarrow \\ 27 \\ +94 \\ \hline \end{array} \qquad \begin{array}{r} \downarrow \\ 58 \\ +44 \\ \hline \end{array} \qquad \begin{array}{r} \downarrow \\ 24 \\ +87 \\ \hline \end{array}$$

	thousands	hundreds	tens	ones
1629	,			
1815	,			
600	,			
93	,			
1325	,			
1784	,			
1593	,			

	thousands	hundreds	tens	ones
39	,			
1298	,			
820	,			
1315	,			
290	,			
1324	,			
1976	,			

Speed
Drill

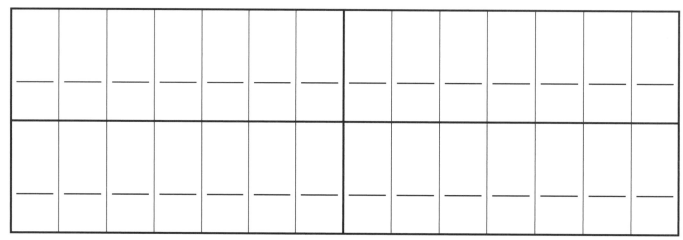

4	12	8	12	8	12
+8	-4	+4	-8	+4	-4

8	4	12	4	12	12
+4	+8	-8	+8	-4	-8

4	12	12	4	12	8	12	8
+8	-8	-4	+8	-8	+4	-4	+4

12	8	12	12	4	12	8	4
-8	+4	-8	-4	+8	-8	+4	+8

"Whatsoever thy hand findeth to do, do it with thy might." Ecclesiastes 9:10

38

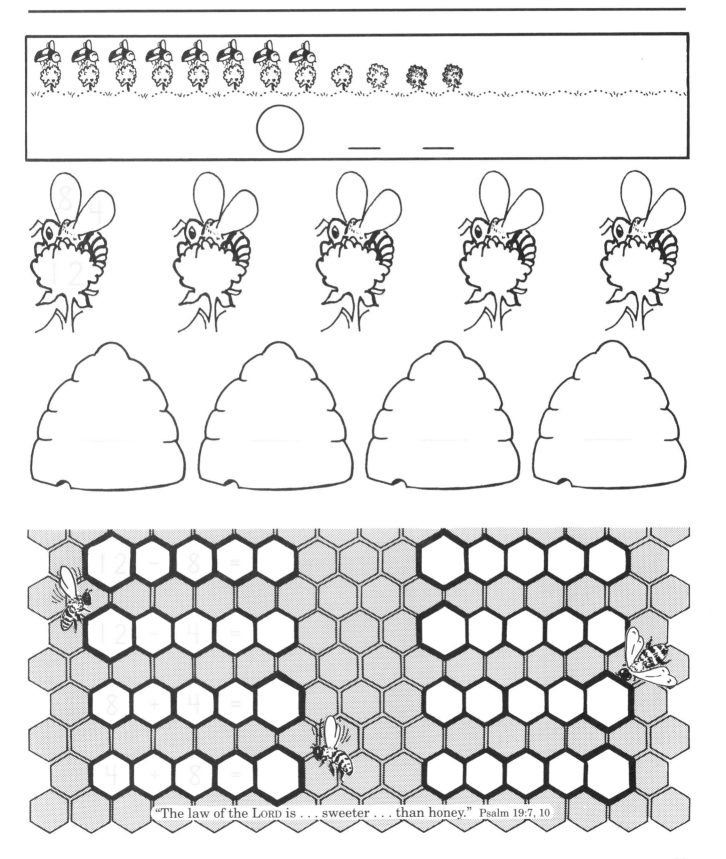

"The law of the LORD is . . . sweeter . . . than honey." Psalm 19:7, 10

$12 - 8 = \underline{}$	$12 - \underline{} = 8$	$\underline{} + 4 = 12$
$12 - 4 = \underline{}$	$\underline{} + 4 = 12$	$\underline{} + 8 = 12$
$4 + \underline{} = 12$	$4 + 8 = \underline{}$	$12 - \underline{} = 4$
$\underline{} - 8 = 4$	$12 - \underline{} = 8$	$\underline{} - 4 = 8$
$8 + \underline{} = 12$	$\underline{} + 4 = 12$	$4 + 8 = \underline{}$
$12 - \underline{} = 4$	$4 + 8 = \underline{}$	$12 - \underline{} = 4$

$$
\begin{array}{cccccccc}
6 & 3 & 4 & 2 & 5 & 2 & 7 & 3 \\
2 & 1 & 3 & 6 & 2 & 2 & 1 & 4 \\
+4 & +8 & +4 & +4 & +4 & +8 & +4 & +3 \\
\hline
\end{array}
$$

$$
\begin{array}{cccccccc}
3 & 1 & 3 & 5 & 4 & 1 & 4 & 2 \\
5 & 3 & 2 & 3 & 1 & 7 & 0 & 4 \\
+4 & +8 & +6 & +4 & +6 & +4 & +8 & +5 \\
\hline
\end{array}
$$

↓	↓	↓	↓	↓	↓
84	35	39	74	27	77
+36	+86	+63	+38	+94	+43

↓	↓	↓	↓	↓	↓
18	66	43	58	24	35
+92	+45	+69	+44	+87	+75

Extra Activity

"His eye seeth every precious thing."
Job 28:10

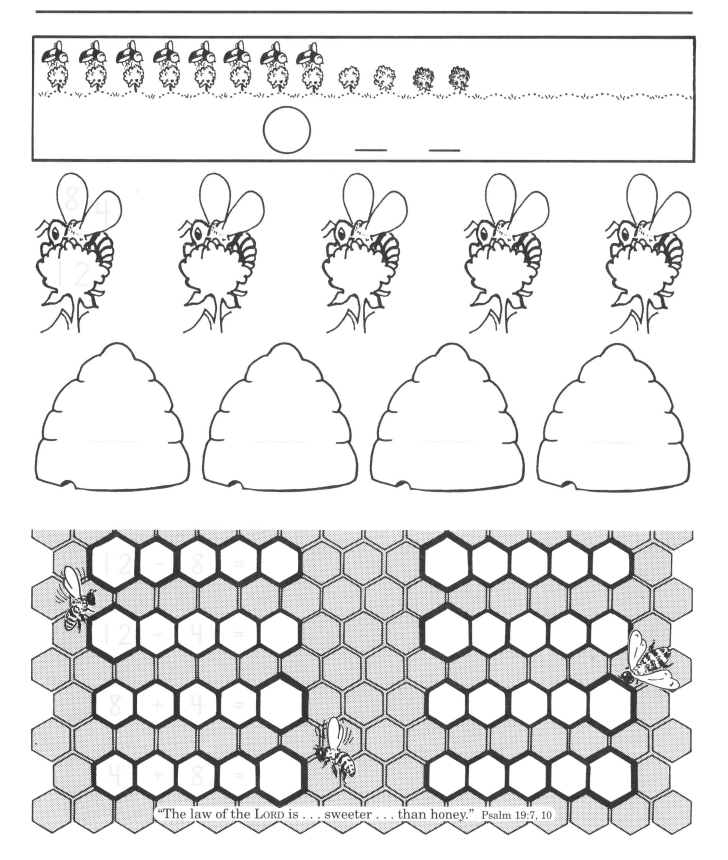

"The law of the LORD is . . . sweeter . . . than honey." Psalm 19:7, 10

Fred has 12 dimes in his bank. He gives four of them to the church. How many dimes are left in his bank?

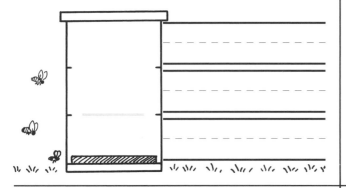

A mouse slips into a hive. 8 bees sting the mouse. Then four more bees sting it. How many bees is that in all?

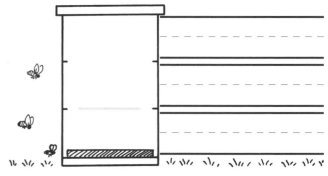

On the way to school Mark saw four trucks with pigs and 8 trucks with hens. How many trucks was that altogether?

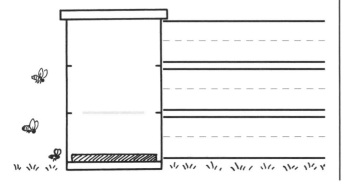

12 children ride in a van. The van stops at school, and 8 children get out. How many children are in the van now?

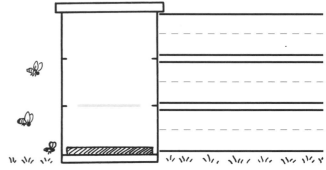

```
  ↓           ↓           ↓           ↓           ↓           ↓
  68          35          84          39          78          96
 +44         +83         +36         +63         +44         +33
_____      _____      _____      _____      _____      _____
```

```
  ↓           ↓           ↓           ↓           ↓           ↓
  83          32          88          44          76          52
 +29         +97         +34         +58         +44         +66
_____      _____      _____      _____      _____      _____
```

```
  54          44          85          53          95          42
  63          30          43          32          32          75
 + 2         + 2         + 1         + 1         + 0         + 2
_____      _____      _____      _____      _____      _____
```

```
  32          82          33          44          23          88
  93          42          51          82          51          40
 + 4         + 3         + 2         + 3         + 2         + 1
_____      _____      _____      _____      _____      _____
```

Speed
Drill

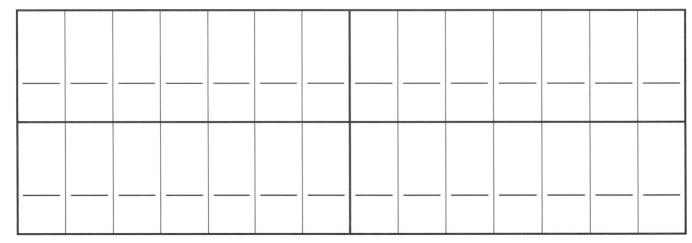

4	12	12	9	12	12
+8	-4	-3	+3	-9	-8

3	12	8	12	9	4
+9	-3	+4	-8	+3	+8

12	4	12	12	3	12	12	8
-4	+8	-8	-9	+9	-3	-4	+4

4	12	8	3	12	4	12	9
+8	-4	+4	+9	-8	+8	-3	+3

"Whatsoever thy hand findeth to do, do it with thy might." Ecclesiastes 9:10

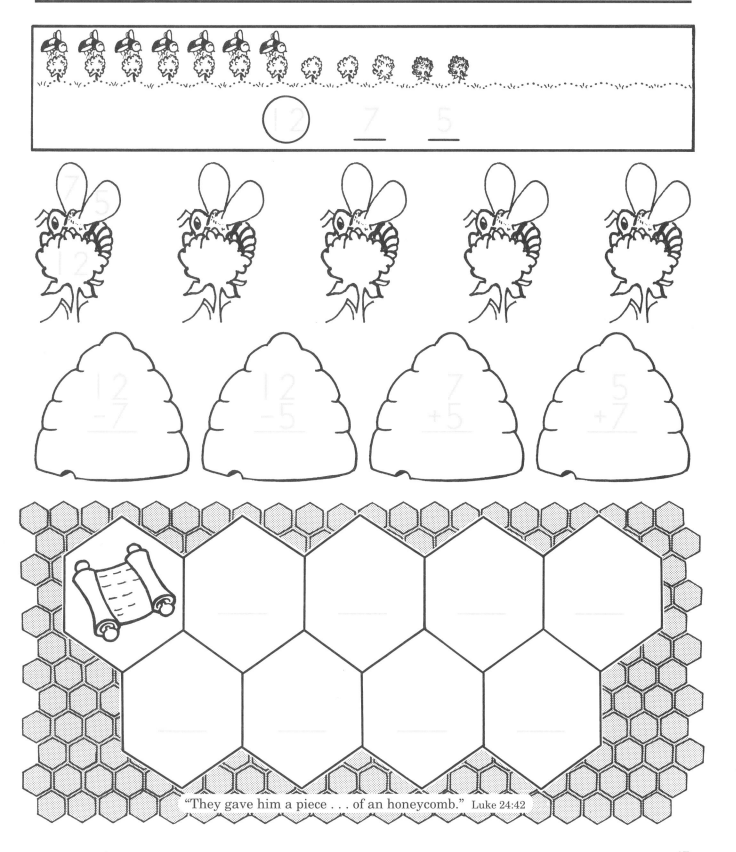

12   7   5

12   12   7   5
−7   −5   +5   +7

"They gave him a piece . . . of an honeycomb." Luke 24:42

5	12	12	7	12	5	12	12
+7	-7	-5	+5	-7	+7	-5	-7

12	7	12	5	12	7	5	12
-5	+5	-7	+7	-5	+5	+7	-7

12	12	7	12	5	12	12	7
-7	-5	+5	-7	+7	-5	-7	+5

12	5	12	7	12	12	5	12
-5	+7	-7	+5	-7	-5	+7	-5

12	12	12	12	12	5	7	12
-7	-5	-7	-5	-7	+7	+5	-7

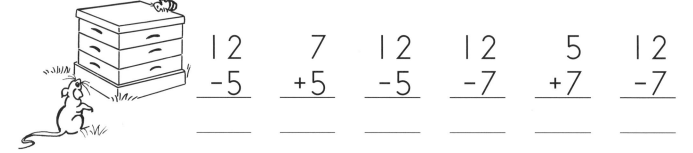

12	7	12	12	5	12
-5	+5	-5	-7	+7	-7

48

$$
\begin{array}{r} 65 \\ +53 \\ \hline \end{array}
\qquad
\begin{array}{r} 54 \\ +48 \\ \hline \end{array}
\qquad
\begin{array}{r} 31 \\ +98 \\ \hline \end{array}
\qquad
\begin{array}{r} 39 \\ +63 \\ \hline \end{array}
\qquad
\begin{array}{r} 77 \\ +43 \\ \hline \end{array}
\qquad
\begin{array}{r} 28 \\ +90 \\ \hline \end{array}
$$

$$
\begin{array}{r} 43 \\ +69 \\ \hline \end{array}
\qquad
\begin{array}{r} 14 \\ +94 \\ \hline \end{array}
\qquad
\begin{array}{r} 78 \\ +44 \\ \hline \end{array}
\qquad
\begin{array}{r} 76 \\ +33 \\ \hline \end{array}
\qquad
\begin{array}{r} 45 \\ +83 \\ \hline \end{array}
\qquad
\begin{array}{r} 35 \\ +75 \\ \hline \end{array}
$$

$$
\begin{array}{r} 79 \\ +43 \\ \hline \end{array}
\qquad
\begin{array}{r} 67 \\ +41 \\ \hline \end{array}
\qquad
\begin{array}{r} 36 \\ +85 \\ \hline \end{array}
\qquad
\begin{array}{r} 55 \\ +53 \\ \hline \end{array}
\qquad
\begin{array}{r} 25 \\ +97 \\ \hline \end{array}
\qquad
\begin{array}{r} 85 \\ +36 \\ \hline \end{array}
$$

"His eye
seeth every
precious thing."

Job 28:10

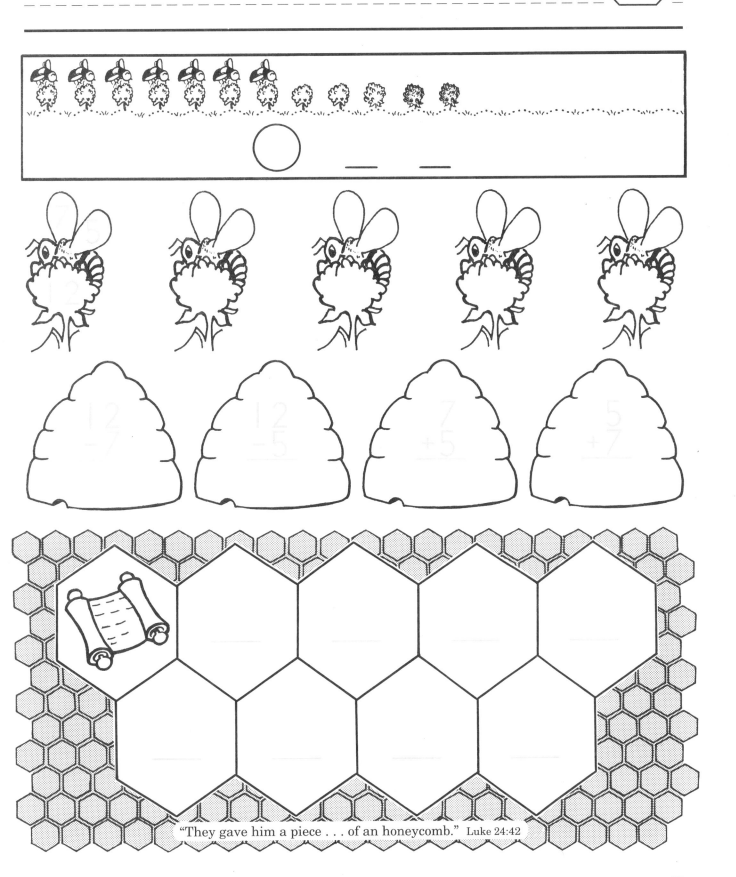

"They gave him a piece . . . of an honeycomb." Luke 24:42

51

```
 121      73     126     125      56     128
 -70     +52     -54     -71     +72     -56
_____   _____   _____   _____   _____   _____


  76     129      52     127      73     127
 +53     -78     +75     -74     +55     -72
_____   _____   _____   _____   _____   _____


  54     128     127     127     129      74
 +71     -77     -73     -55     -57     +54
_____   _____   _____   _____   _____   _____


 127      77     128      54     129      71
 -76     +52     -75     +73     -74     +57
_____   _____   _____   _____   _____   _____


 129      52     128      73      54     128
 -55     +73     -72     +51     +75     -53
_____   _____   _____   _____   _____   _____


                  52     126     129      74
                 +77     -51     -73     +50
                _____   _____   _____   _____
```

52

72

Count by 2's

100			

$$\begin{array}{r} 77 \\ +45 \\ \hline \end{array}$$
$$\begin{array}{r} 67 \\ +41 \\ \hline \end{array}$$
$$\begin{array}{r} 26 \\ +85 \\ \hline \end{array}$$
$$\begin{array}{r} 55 \\ +72 \\ \hline \end{array}$$
$$\begin{array}{r} 65 \\ +57 \\ \hline \end{array}$$
$$\begin{array}{r} 65 \\ +36 \\ \hline \end{array}$$

$$\begin{array}{r} 92 \\ +36 \\ \hline \end{array}$$
$$\begin{array}{r} 48 \\ +54 \\ \hline \end{array}$$
$$\begin{array}{r} 83 \\ +34 \\ \hline \end{array}$$
$$\begin{array}{r} 44 \\ +77 \\ \hline \end{array}$$
$$\begin{array}{r} 87 \\ +34 \\ \hline \end{array}$$
$$\begin{array}{r} 24 \\ +78 \\ \hline \end{array}$$

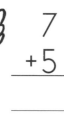

Speed Drill

5 +7	12 -5	7 +5	12 -7	7 +5	12 -5

7 +5	5 +7	12 -7	5 +7	12 -5	12 -7

12 -5	12 -7	12 -5	5 +7	12 -7	7 +5	12 -5	7 +5

12 -7	12 -5	12 -7	12 -5	5 +7	12 -7	7 +5	5 +7

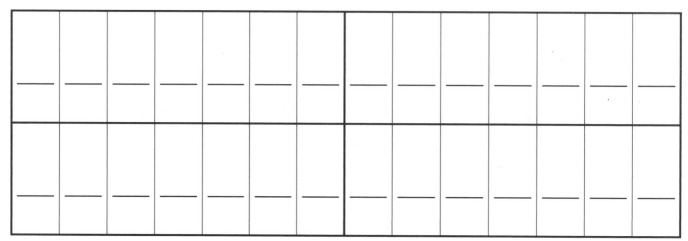

"Whatsoever thy hand findeth to do, do it with thy might." Ecclesiastes 9:10

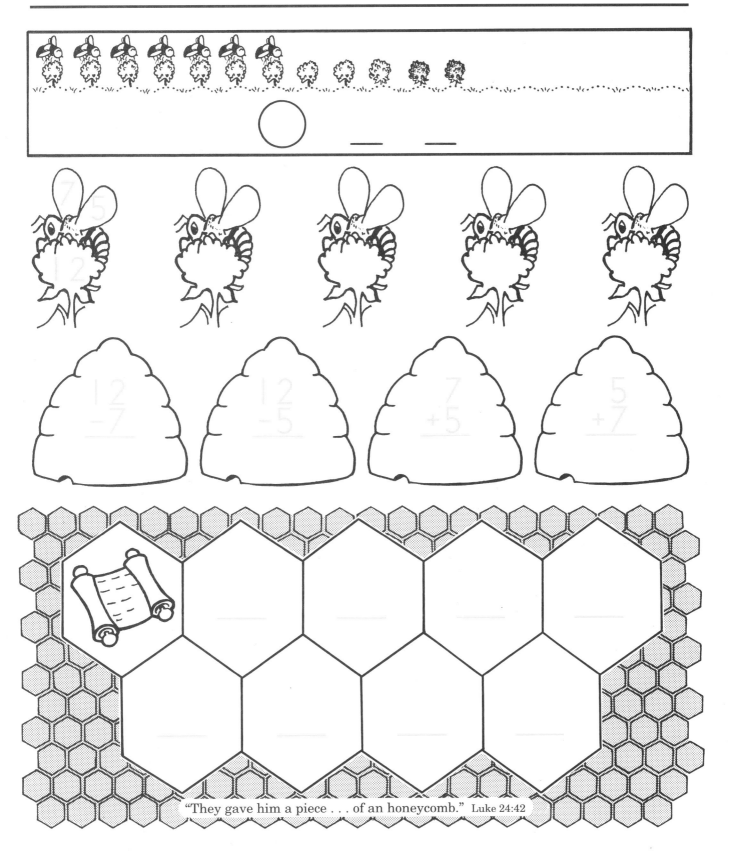

"They gave him a piece . . . of an honeycomb." Luke 24:42

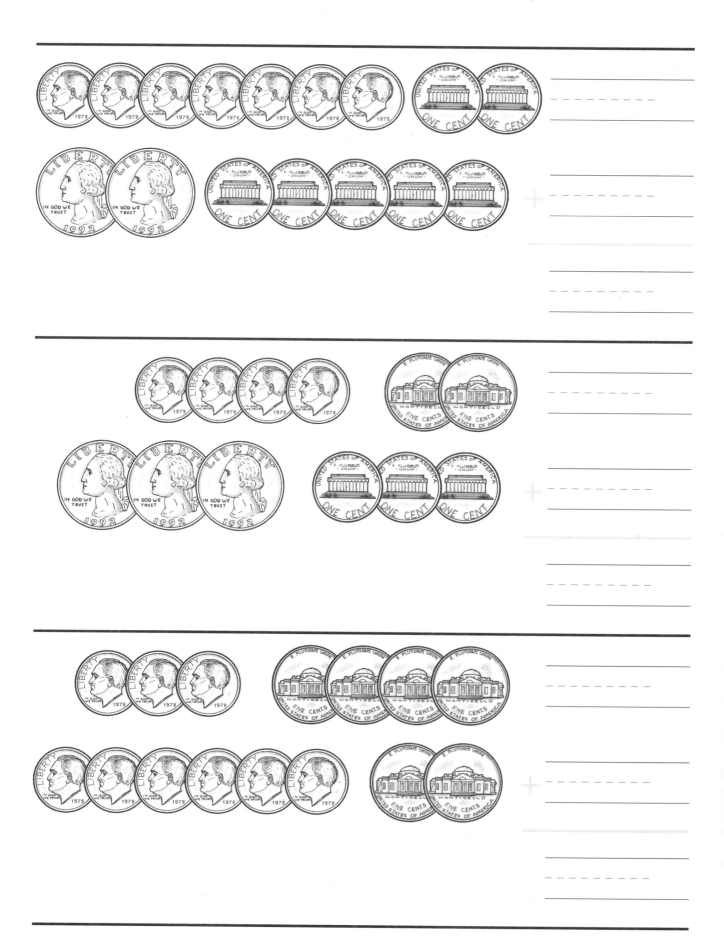

_____

_____

+ _____

_____

_____

_____

+ _____

_____

+ _____

7 +5	12 −8	12 −5	3 +9	12 −4	4 +8	12 −7	12 −3
12 −7	7 +5	12 −9	7 +5	12 −7	5 +7	4 +8	12 −9
12 −3	12 −7	9 +3	12 −4	5 +7	12 −5	12 −8	8 +4

Father read the Bible to blind Mr. Gray. He read 7 verses about Jesus and 5 verses about heaven. How many verses was that?

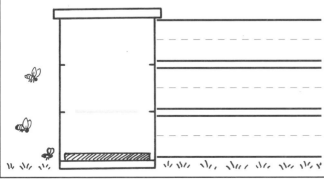

Jay slips 12 coins into his pocket. 7 coins drop out—clink, clink! How many coins are in his pocket now?

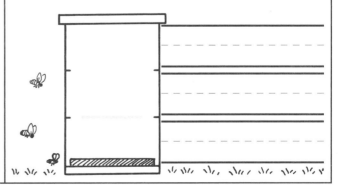

"His eye
seeth every
precious thing."

Job 28:10

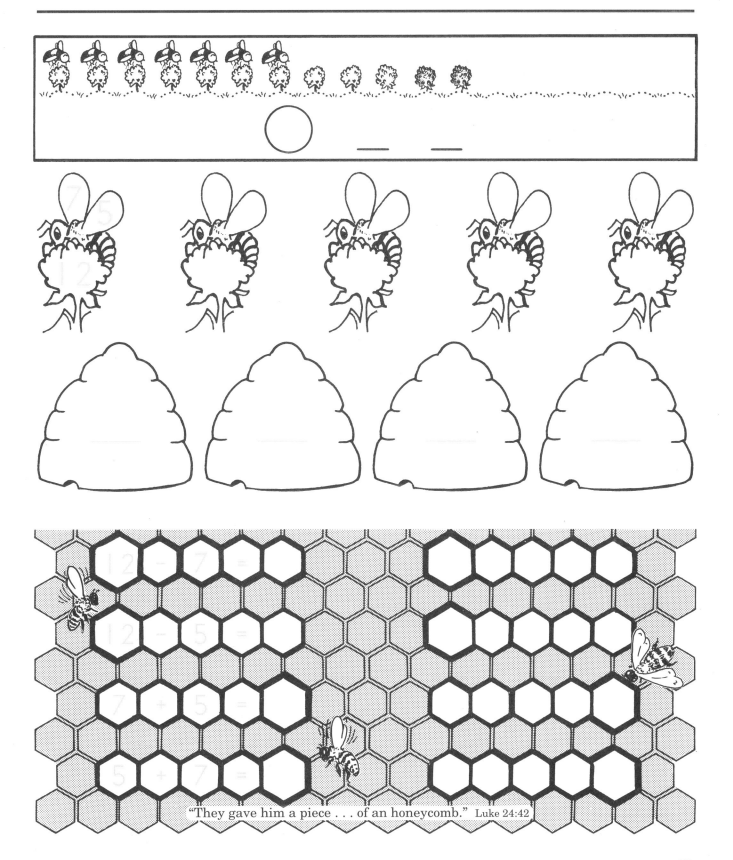

"They gave him a piece . . . of an honeycomb."   Luke 24:42

5 + 7 = ___	12 - ___ = 5	5 + 7 = ___
12 - 7 = ___	12 - 5 = ___	12 - 7 = ___
12 - ___ = 7	7 + 5 = ___	___ - 5 = 7
___ + 5 = 12	5 + ___ = 12	7 + 5 = ___
12 - ___ = 7	___ + 7 = 12	5 + ___ = 12
___ + 5 = 12	12 - ___ = 5	___ - 7 = 5

$$\begin{array}{ccccccc} 6 & 3 & 1 & 4 & 1 & 3 & 5 & 1 \\ 1 & 2 & 6 & 3 & 4 & 2 & 1 & 4 \\ +5 & +5 & +5 & +5 & +6 & +7 & +5 & +7 \\ \hline \end{array}$$

$$\begin{array}{ccccccc} 5 & 1 & 2 & 1 & 5 & 3 & 5 & 4 \\ 2 & 3 & 5 & 6 & 0 & 4 & 4 & 1 \\ +5 & +7 & +5 & +4 & +7 & +5 & +1 & +7 \\ \hline \end{array}$$

	thousands	hundreds	tens	ones
1798	,			
1345	,			
1761	,			
817	,			
1590	,			
1614	,			
62	,			

	thousands	hundreds	tens	ones
89	,			
316	,			
1973	,			
1582	,			
1297	,			
86	,			
1308	,			

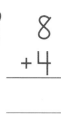

Speed Drill

12	8	7	12	12	3
-5	+4	+5	-7	-4	+9

8	12	9	12	12	12
+4	-5	+3	-8	-7	-9

12	4	5	12	12	3	4	12
-7	+8	+7	-4	-7	+9	+8	-5

12	12	12	12	12	7	12	5
-5	-7	-9	-7	-8	+5	-5	+7

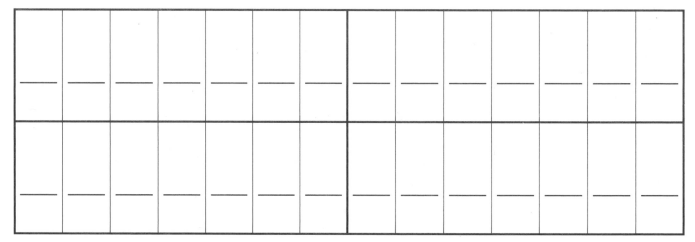

"Whatsoever thy hand findeth to do, do it with thy might." Ecclesiastes 9:10

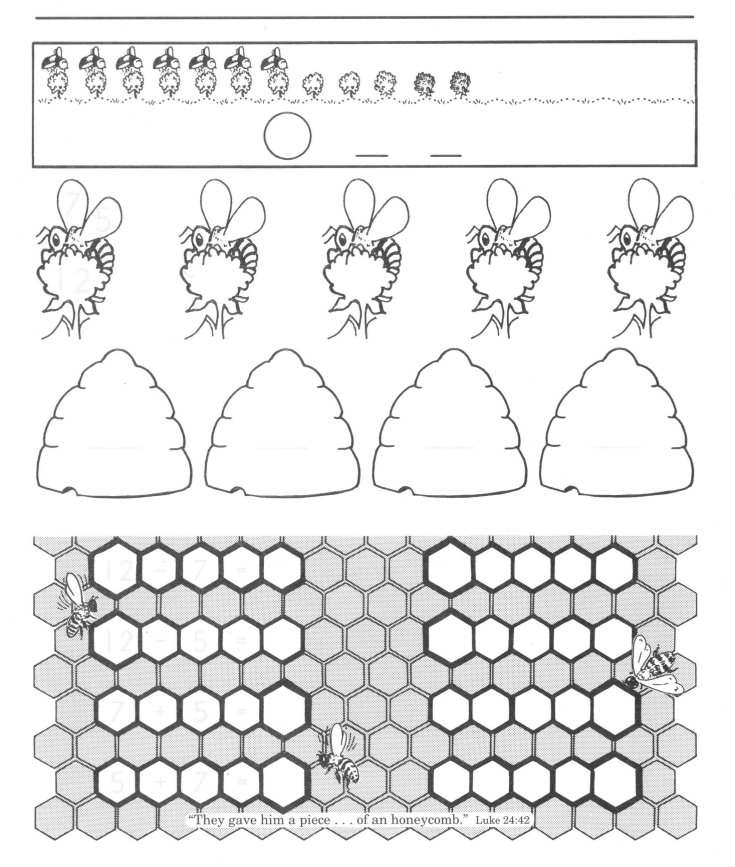

"They gave him a piece . . . of an honeycomb."   Luke 24:42

God sends rain. Splash, splash! Ray splashes in 7 puddles. Fred splashes in 5 puddles. How many puddles is that altogether?

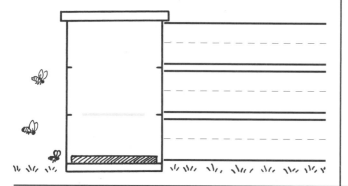

Lee plays with his baby sister. He stacks up 12 blocks. 7 blocks fall down. How many blocks are left on the stack?

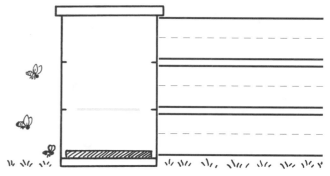

Mother had 12 eggs in a dish. She cooked 5 of them in a pan. How many eggs were left in the dish?

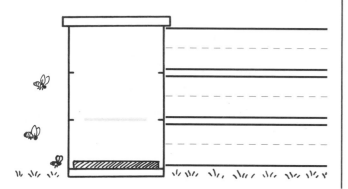

Five cows stand in the creek. 7 cows eat grass. How many cows is that?

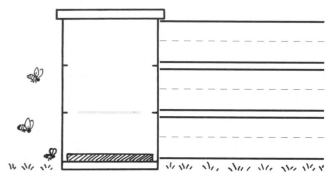

$$
\begin{array}{r} 8 \\ +4 \\ \hline \end{array}
\qquad
\begin{array}{r} 12 \\ -7 \\ \hline \end{array}
\qquad
\begin{array}{r} 12 \\ -3 \\ \hline \end{array}
\qquad
\begin{array}{r} 6 \\ +5 \\ \hline \end{array}
\qquad
\begin{array}{r} 11 \\ -5 \\ \hline \end{array}
\qquad
\begin{array}{r} 7 \\ +5 \\ \hline \end{array}
\qquad
\begin{array}{r} 12 \\ -8 \\ \hline \end{array}
\qquad
\begin{array}{r} 12 \\ -5 \\ \hline \end{array}
$$

$$
\begin{array}{r} 12 \\ -4 \\ \hline \end{array}
\qquad
\begin{array}{r} 6 \\ +5 \\ \hline \end{array}
\qquad
\begin{array}{r} 12 \\ -7 \\ \hline \end{array}
\qquad
\begin{array}{r} 5 \\ +6 \\ \hline \end{array}
\qquad
\begin{array}{r} 12 \\ -4 \\ \hline \end{array}
\qquad
\begin{array}{r} 5 \\ +7 \\ \hline \end{array}
\qquad
\begin{array}{r} 9 \\ +3 \\ \hline \end{array}
\qquad
\begin{array}{r} 12 \\ -7 \\ \hline \end{array}
$$

$$
\begin{array}{r} 12 \\ -5 \\ \hline \end{array}
\qquad
\begin{array}{r} 12 \\ -8 \\ \hline \end{array}
\qquad
\begin{array}{r} 5 \\ +7 \\ \hline \end{array}
\qquad
\begin{array}{r} 11 \\ -5 \\ \hline \end{array}
\qquad
\begin{array}{r} 5 \\ +6 \\ \hline \end{array}
\qquad
\begin{array}{r} 12 \\ -3 \\ \hline \end{array}
\qquad
\begin{array}{r} 12 \\ -7 \\ \hline \end{array}
\qquad
\begin{array}{r} 4 \\ +8 \\ \hline \end{array}
$$

"His eye
seeth every
precious thing."

Job 28:10

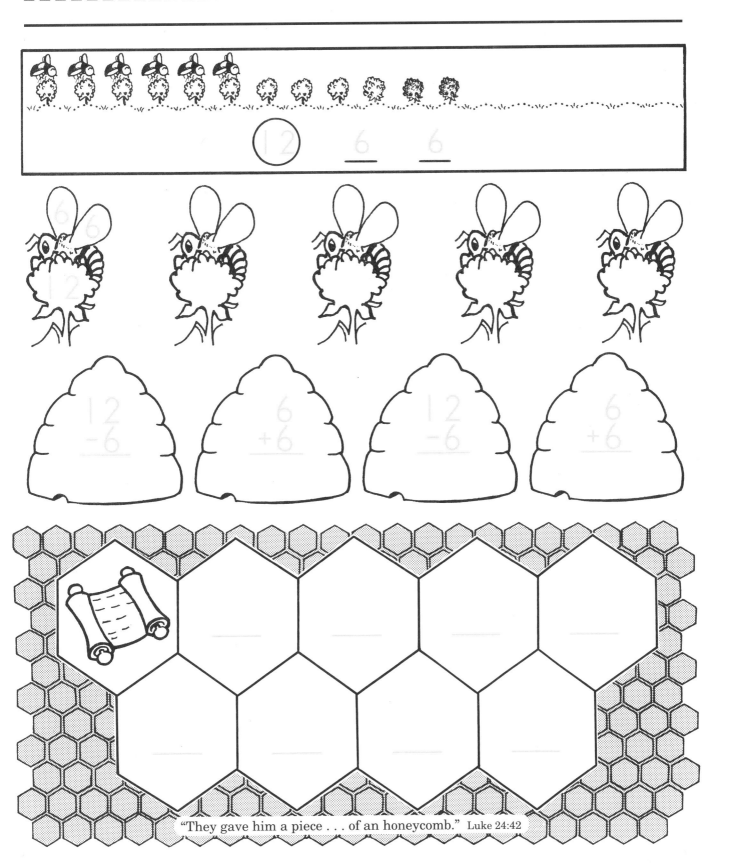

"They gave him a piece . . . of an honeycomb." Luke 24:42

6	11	12	6	11	5	12	11
+6	−5	−6	+5	−6	+6	−6	−6

12	6	11	6	12	6	5	11
−6	+6	−6	+6	−6	+5	+6	−6

11	12	6	11	5	11	12	6
−6	−6	+5	−6	+6	−5	−6	+6

12	6	12	5	12	11	6	11
−6	+6	−6	+6	−6	−6	+6	−5

12	11	11	12	11	6	6	11
−6	−6	−5	−6	−5	+6	+6	−5

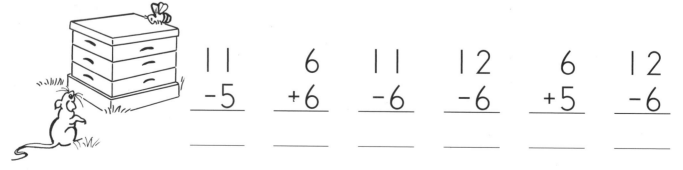

11	6	11	12	6	12
−5	+6	−6	−6	+5	−6

57 +45	77 +51	86 +35	52 +65	65 +57	55 +46
72 +36	28 +94	53 +74	74 +37	87 +34	64 +38
79 +43	67 +41	36 +85	55 +53	25 +97	85 +36

Speed
Drill

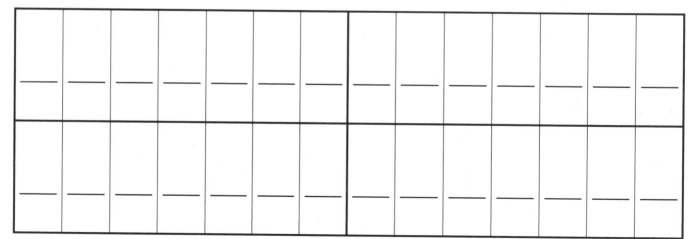

6	12	6	11	11	5
+6	-6	+5	-5	-6	+6

11	6	11	6	12	11
-5	+6	-6	+5	-6	-5

5	6	6	11	12	5	11	6
+6	+6	+5	-6	-6	+6	-5	+6

6	5	12	11	6	11	6	12
+6	+6	-6	-5	+5	-6	+6	-6

"Whatsoever thy hand findeth to do, do it with thy might." Ecclesiastes 9:10

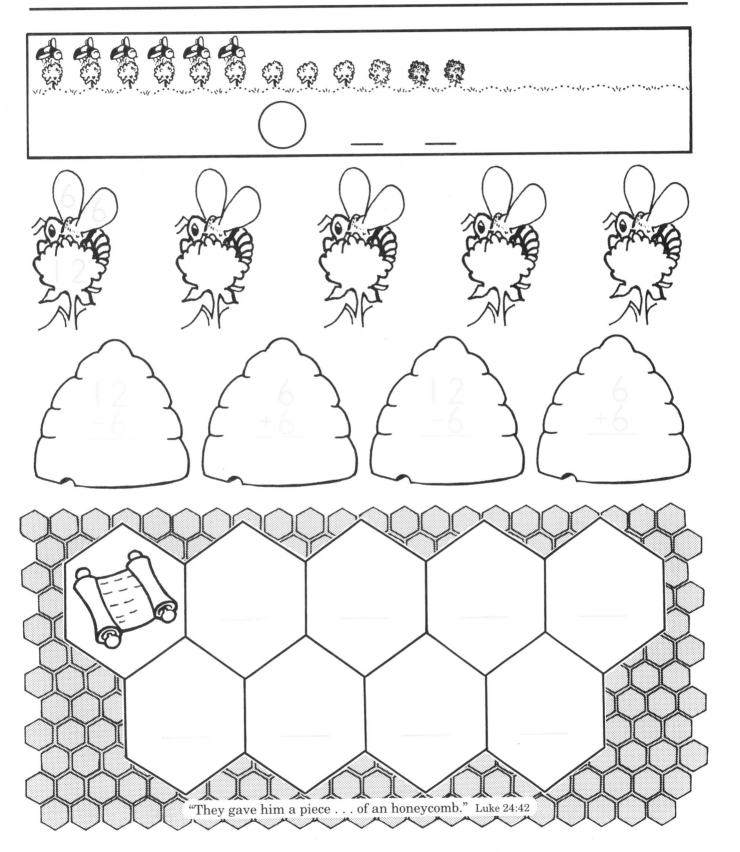

"They gave him a piece . . . of an honeycomb." Luke 24:42

```
    61        123        53         67        113        57
  +62        -62       +64        +61        -53       +62
  ____       ____      ____       ____       ____      ____


   129        119        65        129         66        119
   -67        -63       +61        -61        +60        -65
  ____       ____      ____       ____       ____      ____


    65        114        65         65        129         63
   +54        -54       +63        +52        -68        +60
  ____       ____      ____       ____       ____      ____


   118        127       118         61        129         66
   -55        -64       -67        +57        -67        +63
  ____       ____      ____       ____       ____      ____


    61        118        61        128         64        118
   +68        -64       +65        -60        +62        -62
  ____       ____      ____       ____       ____      ____
```

```
              127         62        118        125
              -65        +56        -67        -62
             ____       ____       ____       ____
```

6 +6	12 -7	12 -6	7 +5	12 -4	6 +6	12 -8	12 -5

12 -9	8 +4	12 -7	3 +9	12 -9	9 +3	4 +8	12 -7

12 -5	12 -8	3 +9	12 -4	5 +7	12 -6	12 -7	6 +6

"His eye
seeth every
precious thing."

Job 28:10

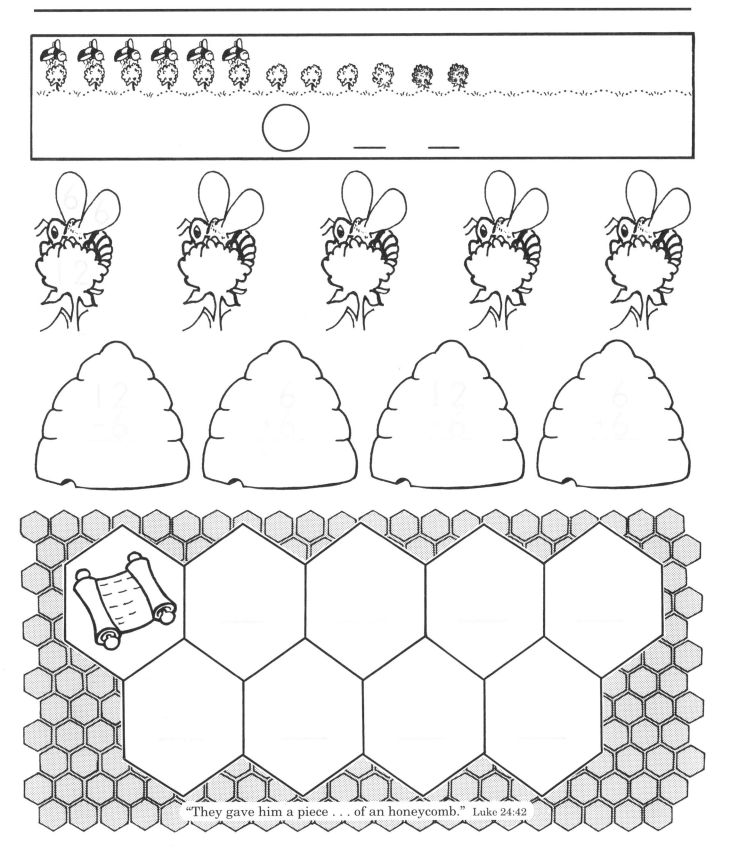

"They gave him a piece . . . of an honeycomb." Luke 24:42

Father took 12 Bibles to a jail. He gave six Bibles to some of the men. How many Bibles did Father have then?

Jay and Ray helped Father cut corn. Jay cut six rows. Ray cut six rows. How many rows did **both** boys cut?

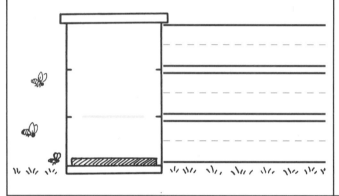
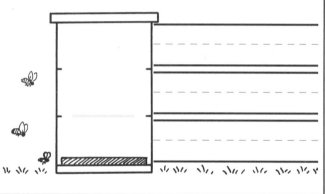

$$
\begin{array}{ccccccc}
3 & 3 & 2 & 4 & 2 & 1 & 3 & 6 \\
3 & 5 & 1 & 2 & 4 & 4 & 4 & 1 \\
+6 & +4 & +8 & +5 & +6 & +6 & +3 & +5 \\
\hline
\end{array}
$$

$$
\begin{array}{ccccccc}
3 & 2 & 2 & 5 & 2 & 5 & 4 & 1 \\
2 & 2 & 4 & 1 & 5 & 1 & 2 & 5 \\
+7 & +6 & +5 & +6 & +4 & +5 & +6 & +6 \\
\hline
\end{array}
$$

```
 82      86      92      54      55      74
+43     +26     +36     +48     +57     +32
----    ----    ----    ----    ----    ----


 77      21      63      78      83      68
+45     +94     +59     +30     +33     +34
----    ----    ----    ----    ----    ----


 96      84      36      55      25      42
+32     +43     +86     +73     +97     +85
----    ----    ----    ----    ----    ----
```

6	12	6	11	11	5
+6	−6	+5	−5	−6	+6

11	6	11	6	12	11
−5	+6	−6	+5	−6	−5

5	6	6	11	12	5	11	6
+6	+6	+5	−6	−6	+6	−5	+6

6	5	12	11	6	11	6	12
+6	+6	−6	−5	+5	−6	+6	−6

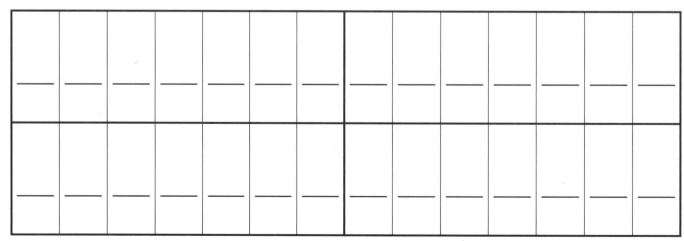

"Whatsoever thy hand findeth to do, do it with thy might." Ecclesiastes 9:10

78

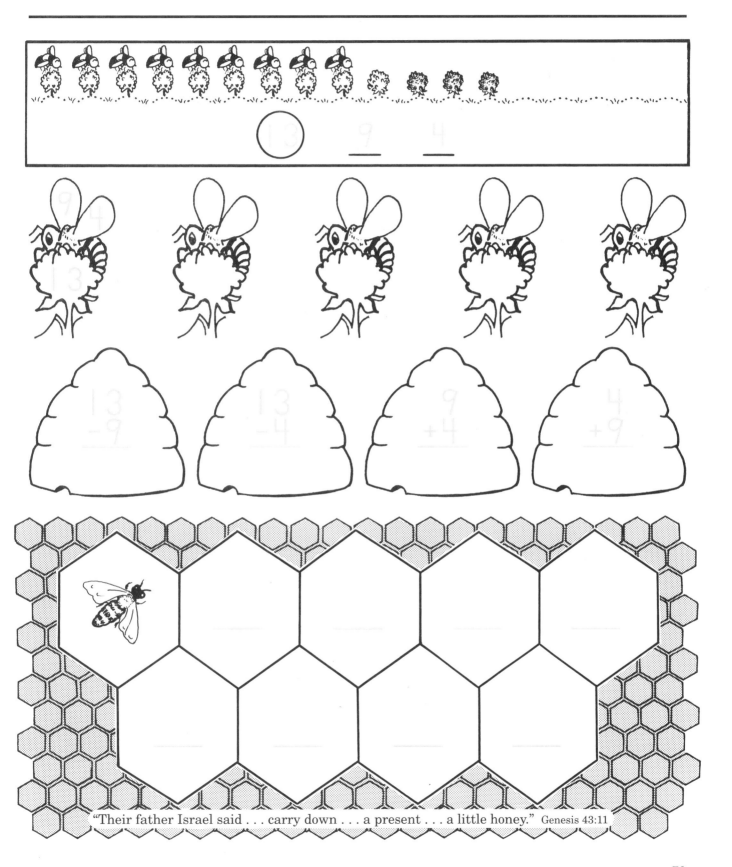

13   9   4

13   13   9   4
−9   −4   +4   +9

"Their father Israel said . . . carry down . . . a present . . . a little honey." Genesis 43:11

13	13	13	13	4	13	13	9
-9	-4	-9	-9	+9	-9	-4	+4

4	13	9	4	13	9	13	13
+9	-4	+4	+9	-4	+4	-4	-9

13	13	9	13	9	4	13	4
-9	-4	+4	-4	+4	+9	-4	+9

9	4	13	4	13	13	9	13
+4	+9	-4	+9	-9	-4	+4	-9

13	13	13	13	4	13	13	9
-9	-4	-9	-9	+9	-9	-4	+4

4	13	9	13	4	13
+9	-4	+4	-4	+9	-9

 Count by

2's

100			

81

"His eye
seeth every
precious thing."

Job 28:10

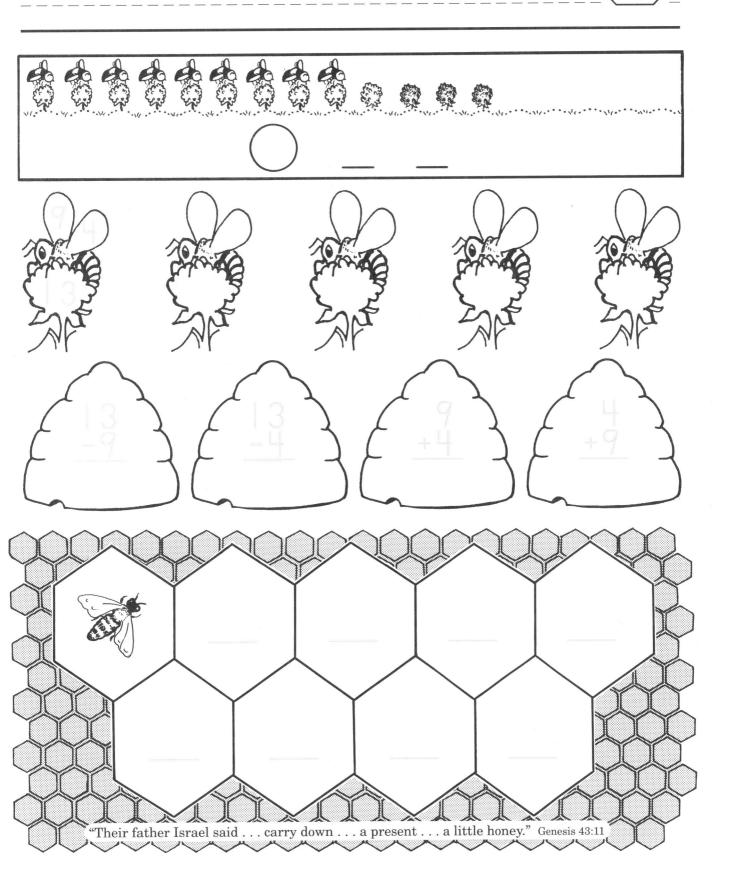

$\bigcirc$ ___ ___

$\begin{array}{r} 13 \\ -\ 9 \\ \hline \end{array}$ $\begin{array}{r} 13 \\ -\ 4 \\ \hline \end{array}$ $\begin{array}{r} 9 \\ +\ 4 \\ \hline \end{array}$ $\begin{array}{r} 4 \\ +\ 9 \\ \hline \end{array}$

"Their father Israel said . . . carry down . . . a present . . . a little honey." Genesis 43:11

13 −4	13 −9	13 −4	13 −4	4 +9	13 −4	13 −9	9 +4
9 +4	13 −4	9 +4	4 +9	13 −9	9 +4	13 −4	13 −9
13 −9	13 −4	9 +4	13 −9	9 +4	4 +9	13 −4	4 +9
4 +9	9 +4	13 −4	4 +9	13 −9	13 −4	9 +4	13 −9
13 −9	13 −4	13 −9	13 −9	4 +9	13 −9	13 −4	9 +4

		9 +4	13 −4	4 +9	13 −4	4 +9	13 −4

92 +43	86 +26	89 +44	54 +48	55 +57	44 +94
42 +90	63 +52	33 +99	64 +39	83 +35	38 +94
74 +29	84 +43	66 +56	62 +41	25 +97	42 +85

God sent snow. He sent nine inches on Sunday and four inches on Monday. How many inches did He send on **both** days?

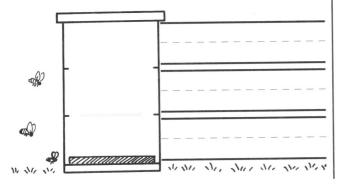

Carl looked for rabbit tracks in the snow. He saw 4 tracks on a hill and 9 tracks in the woods. How many tracks was that?

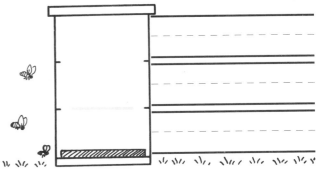

Speed
Drill

13	13	13	4	13	9
-9	-4	-9	+9	-9	+4

4	13	9	4	13	13
+9	-9	+4	+9	-4	-9

13	9	4	13	9	13	13	13
-9	+4	+9	-9	+4	-9	-4	-9

4	13	13	13	9	4	13	9
+9	-9	-9	-4	+4	+9	-9	+4

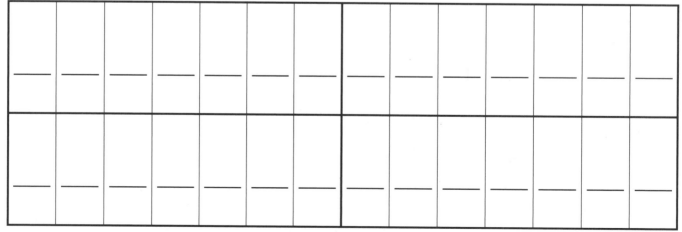

"Whatsoever thy hand findeth to do, do it with thy might." Ecclesiastes 9:10

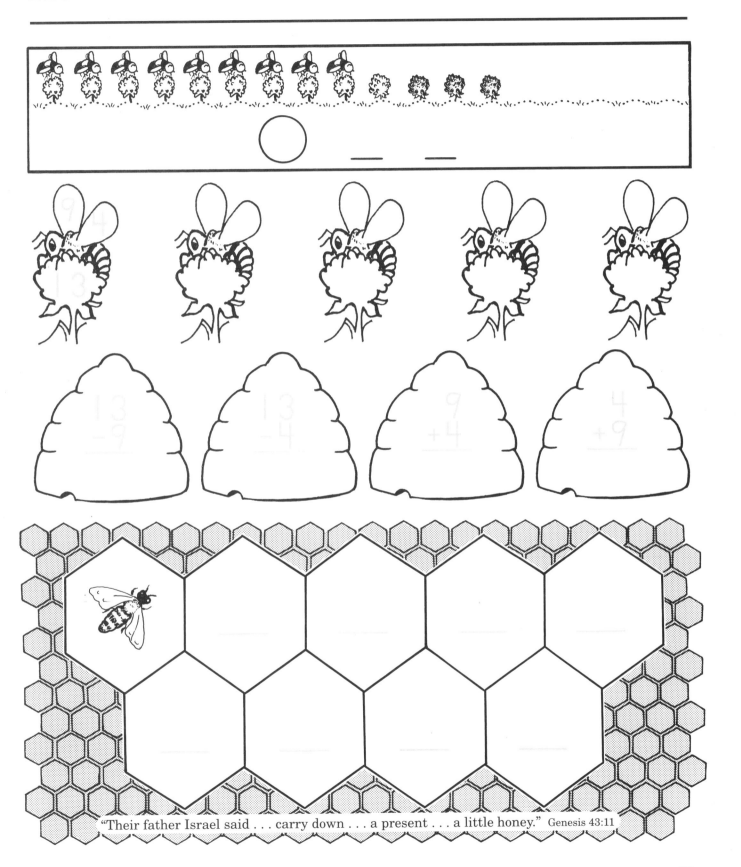

"Their father Israel said . . . carry down . . . a present . . . a little honey." Genesis 43:11

139	39	137	136	96	138
-92	+44	-45	-94	+43	-96

34	139	95	139	39	133
+69	-46	+42	-94	+24	-43

44	138	134	135	139	94
+39	-91	-92	-43	-97	+45

138	59	135	43	137	39
-45	+44	-90	+94	-47	+24

138	74	138	93	29	139
-93	+19	-44	+45	+74	-98

44	137	29	137
+94	-43	+64	-92

	thousands	hundreds	tens	ones
1297	____ ,	____	____	____
1389	____ ,	____	____	____
1973	____ ,	____	____	____
798	____ ,	____	____	____
1316	____ ,	____	____	____
1864	____ ,	____	____	____
62	____ ,	____	____	____

	thousands	hundreds	tens	ones
45	____ ,	____	____	____
590	____ ,	____	____	____
1614	____ ,	____	____	____
1582	____ ,	____	____	____
1297	____ ,	____	____	____
761	____ ,	____	____	____
1308	____ ,	____	____	____

"His eye
seeth every
precious thing."

Job 28:10

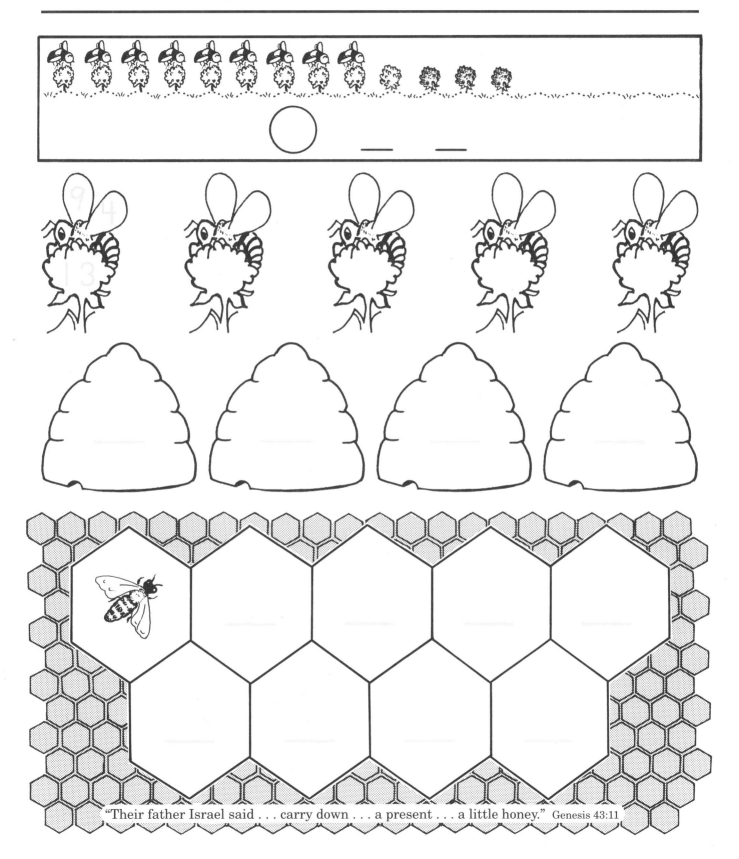

"Their father Israel said . . . carry down . . . a present . . . a little honey." Genesis 43:11

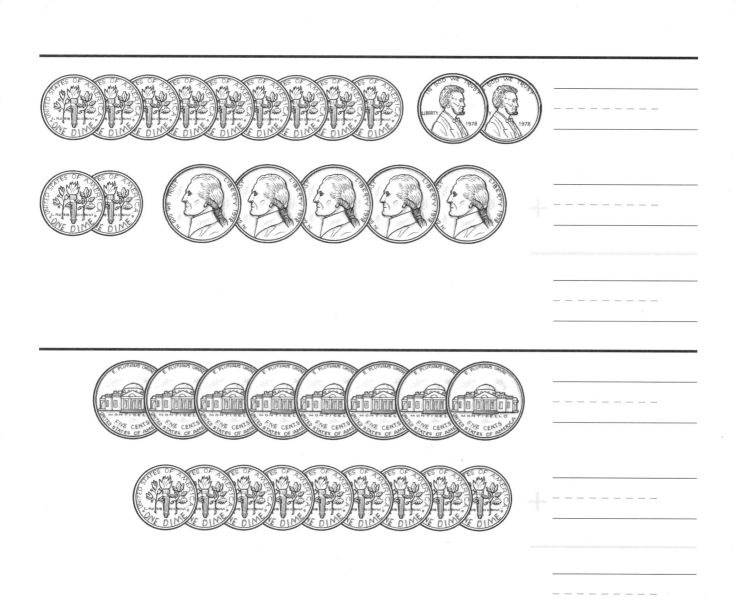

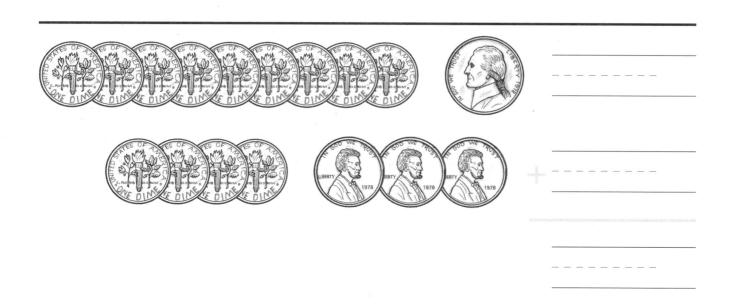

9 +4	12 −7	13 −9	7 +5	12 −6	4 +9	13 −4	12 −5

13 −9	6 +6	13 −4	5 +7	13 −9	9 +4	4 +9	13 −4

12 −5	13 −4	9 +4	12 −6	5 +7	13 −9	12 −7	9 +4

Speed
Drill

13	12	12	13	4	13
-4	-3	-9	-9	+9	-9

9	12	9	3	13	12
+3	-3	+4	+9	-9	-9

9	3	13	4	13	12	13	12
+4	+9	-9	+9	-9	-9	-4	-3

9	4	12	13	3	9	13	9
+3	+9	-9	-9	+9	+4	-4	+3

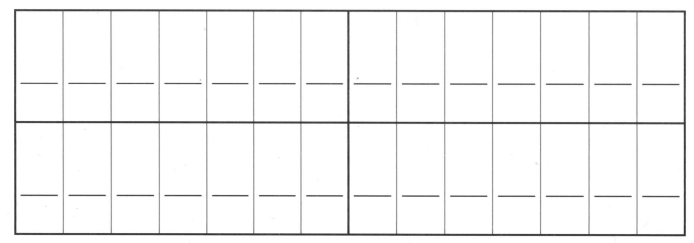

"Whatsoever thy hand findeth to do, do it with thy might." Ecclesiastes 9:10

94

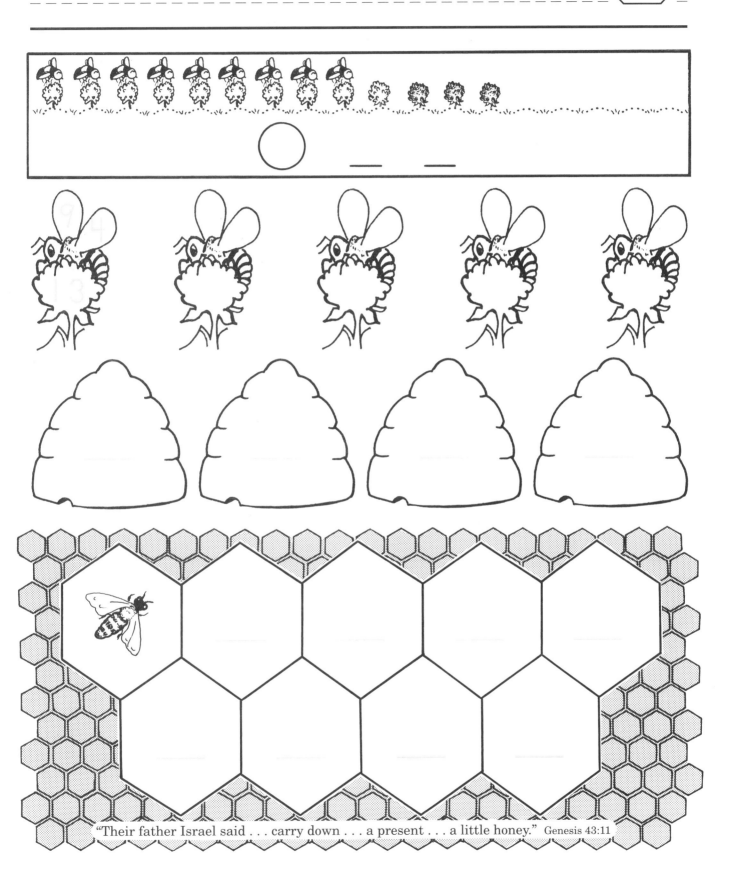

"Their father Israel said . . . carry down . . . a present . . . a little honey." Genesis 43:11

$9 + \underline{} = 13$	$13 - \underline{} = 4$	$\underline{} - 4 = 9$
$4 + \underline{} = 13$	$\underline{} + 9 = 13$	$4 + \underline{} = 13$
$13 - \underline{} = 4$	$\underline{} - 9 = 4$	$13 - 9 = \underline{}$
$13 - \underline{} = 9$	$13 - 4 = \underline{}$	$\underline{} - 4 = 9$
$\underline{} + 9 = 13$	$4 + \underline{} = 13$	$4 + \underline{} = 13$
$\underline{} - 9 = 4$	$9 + 4 = \underline{}$	$\underline{} - 9 = 4$

$$\begin{array}{cccccccc} 6 & 3 & 4 & 3 & 8 & 2 & 4 & 1 \\ 3 & 2 & 5 & 5 & 1 & 7 & 3 & 1 \\ \underline{+4} & \underline{+7} & \underline{+4} & \underline{+2} & \underline{+4} & \underline{+4} & \underline{+5} & \underline{+9} \\ \hline \end{array}$$

$$\begin{array}{cccccccc} 5 & 2 & 7 & 3 & 5 & 2 & 1 & 2 \\ 4 & 2 & 2 & 6 & 3 & 2 & 6 & 2 \\ \underline{+2} & \underline{+6} & \underline{+4} & \underline{+4} & \underline{+2} & \underline{+9} & \underline{+3} & \underline{+9} \\ \hline \end{array}$$

34 +69	139 -46	95 +42	139 -94	49 +54	138 -45
139 -97	74 +49	138 -44	93 +45	29 +74	139 -98
136 -95	74 +29	46 +92	137 -43	69 +54	137 -95

"His eye
seeth every
precious thing."

Job 28:10

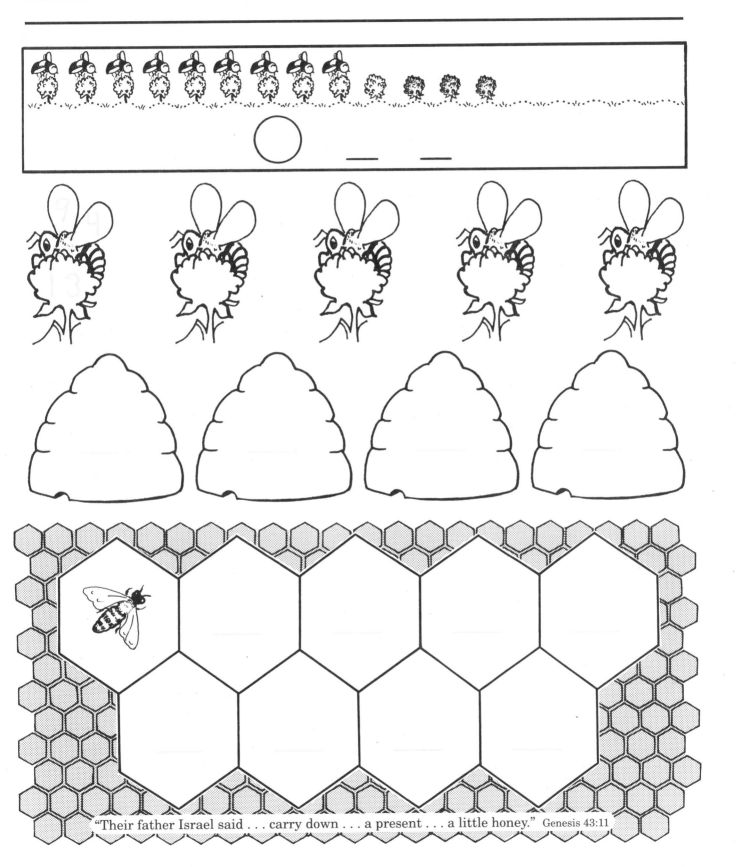

"Their father Israel said . . . carry down . . . a present . . . a little honey." Genesis 43:11

Father does not work on Sunday. He is at church for 4 hours. He reads, and he visits the sick for 7 hours. How many hours is that?

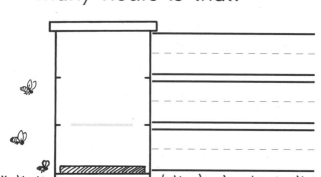

Father had 13 hogs. On Friday he took nine of them to market. How many hogs did Father have then?

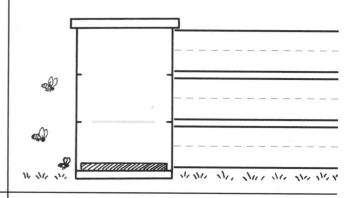

Father makes a bird feeder. Tap, tap! Lee gives 9 nails to Father. Roy gives 4 nails. How many nails do **both** boys give?

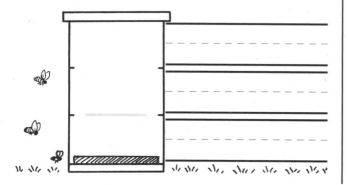

Mae looks at God's pretty snow-flakes. She catches 13 flakes on her coat. Four flakes melt. How many flakes are left?

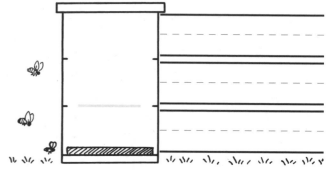

```
  45        52        35        55        44        61
  23        37        43        32        42        25
 +52       +42       +51       +25       +45       +42
 ────      ────      ────      ────      ────      ────


  92        32        63        44        23        45
  43        17        61        92        26        80
 + 4       + 3       + 2       + 3       + 3       + 1
 ────      ────      ────      ────      ────      ────


  14        44        35        56        24        74
  23        34        43        12        14        15
 +94       +42       +34       +61       +90       +42
 ────      ────      ────      ────      ────      ────
```

Write **C** in each **circle**.

Write **S** in each **square**.

Speed
Drill

$$\begin{array}{cccccc} 13 & 12 & 12 & 12 & 13 & 12 \\ -9 & -6 & -5 & -8 & -9 & -3 \\ \hline \end{array}$$

$$\begin{array}{cccccc} 11 & 12 & 11 & 12 & 13 & 11 \\ -5 & -8 & -5 & -5 & -4 & -2 \\ \hline \end{array}$$

$$\begin{array}{cccccccc} 11 & 13 & 12 & 11 & 12 & 11 & 12 & 13 \\ -4 & -4 & -3 & -7 & -8 & -4 & -6 & -9 \\ \hline \end{array}$$

$$\begin{array}{cccccccc} 13 & 12 & 11 & 13 & 12 & 12 & 13 & 11 \\ -4 & -5 & -2 & -4 & -5 & -6 & -9 & -5 \\ \hline \end{array}$$

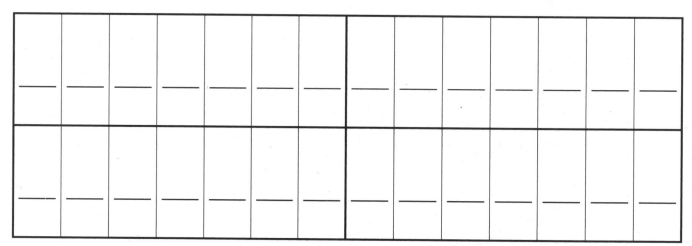

"Whatsoever thy hand findeth to do, do it with thy might." Ecclesiastes 9:10

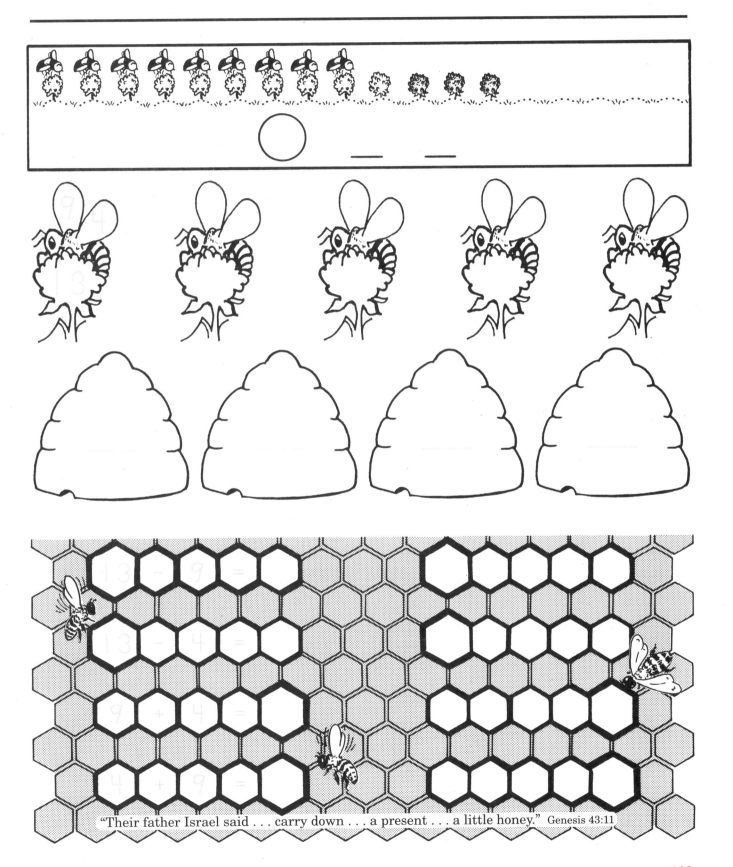

"Their father Israel said . . . carry down . . . a present . . . a little honey." Genesis 43:11

13	12	13	13	9	13	12	9
-9	-3	-4	-9	+4	-4	-3	+4

4	13	3	4	13	9	13	13
+9	-4	+9	+9	-9	+3	-4	-9

12	12	4	12	9	9	12	3
-9	-3	+9	-9	+3	+4	-3	+9

9	4	13	3	12	13	9	12
+3	+9	-9	+9	-9	-9	+4	-9

13	12	13	13	12	13	12	3
-9	-3	-9	-4	-9	-9	-3	+9

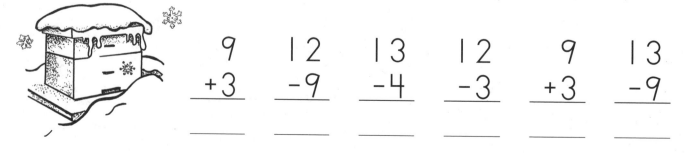

	9	12	13	12	9	13
	+3	-9	-4	-3	+3	-9

104

Write **S** in each **square**.

Write **T** in each **triangle**.

     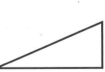

     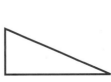

"His eye
seeth every
precious thing."

Job 28:10

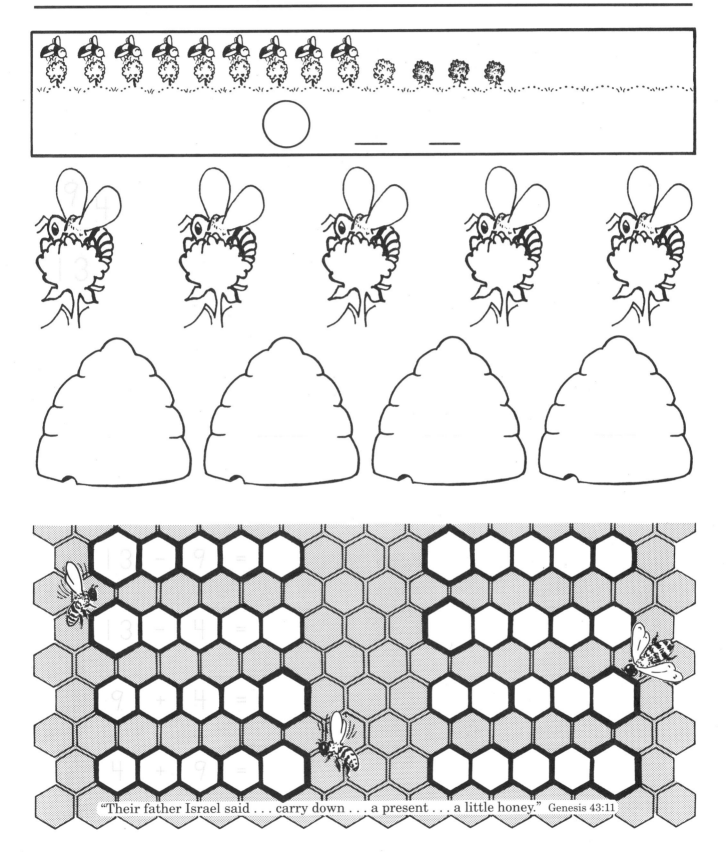

"Their father Israel said . . . carry down . . . a present . . . a little honey." Genesis 43:11

13 −9	11 −2	12 −8	13 −9	8 +4	11 −7	12 −3	3 +9
4 +9	12 −9	6 +5	9 +4	11 −7	5 +6	12 −9	12 −8
12 −6	11 −8	4 +9	11 −5	6 +6	9 +4	12 −9	7 +5
8 +3	3 +9	12 −7	9 +2	11 −9	11 −6	5 +7	11 −9
11 −3	13 −4	11 −4	12 −4	4 +9	12 −5	11 −2	9 +4

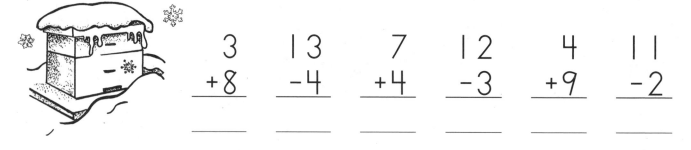

3 +8	13 −4	7 +4	12 −3	4 +9	11 −2

108

| Write **C** in each **circle**. |
| Write **S** in each **square**. |
| Write **T** in each **triangle**. |

  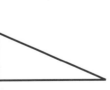   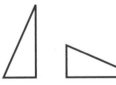 

9	7	3	8	9	4
+4	+5	+8	+4	+3	+9

9	8	4	6	2	9
+3	+4	+9	+5	+9	+4

6	5	9	3	6	8	3	4
+6	+6	+4	+9	+6	+3	+9	+9

9	4	4	6	4	9	5	6
+2	+8	+9	+5	+7	+4	+7	+6

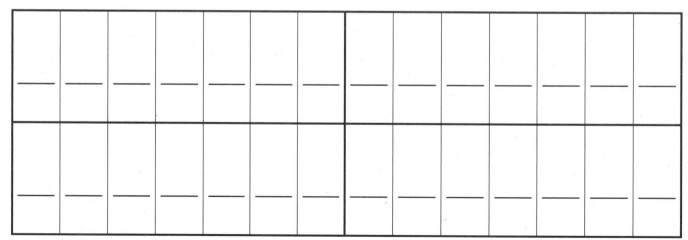

"Whatsoever thy hand findeth to do, do it with thy might." Ecclesiastes 9:10

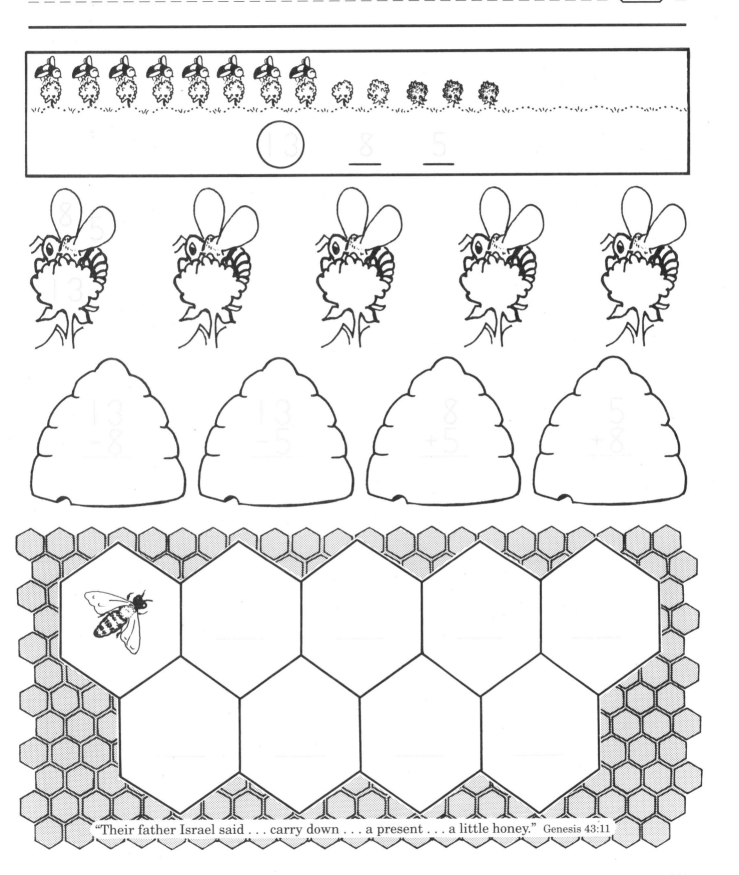

"Their father Israel said . . . carry down . . . a present . . . a little honey." Genesis 43:11

13	13	13	13	5	13	13	8
−8	−8	−5	−8	+8	−5	−8	+5

5	13	8	5	13	8	13	13
+8	−5	+5	+8	−5	+5	−5	−5

13	13	5	13	8	5	13	5
−8	−5	+8	−5	+5	+8	−5	+8

8	5	13	5	13	13	8	13
+5	+8	−8	+8	−5	−8	+5	−5

13	13	13	13	8	13	13	5
−8	−5	−8	−5	+5	−8	−5	+8

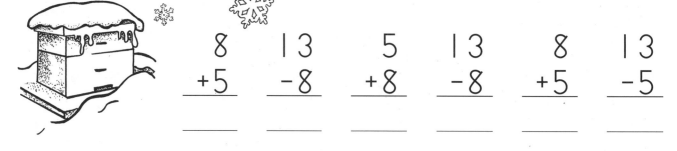

	8	13	5	13	8	13
	+5	−8	+8	−8	+5	−5

_____ _____ _____ _____ _____

_____ _____ _____ _____ _____

Write **S** in each **square**.

Write **R** in each **rectangle**.

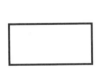   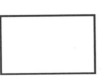  

       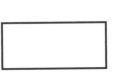

"His eye seeth every precious thing."

Job 28:10

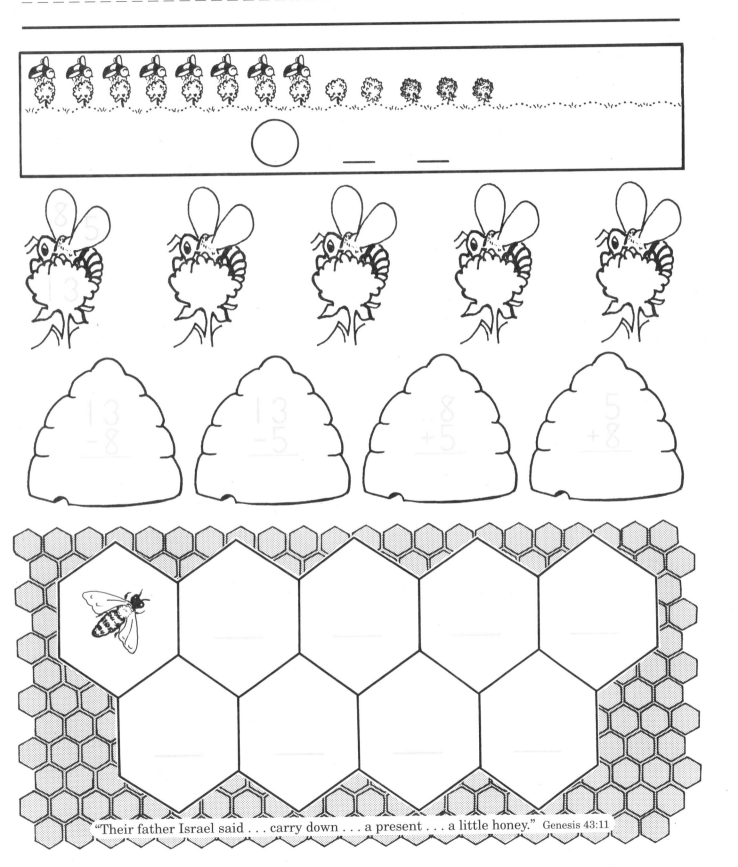

"Their father Israel said . . . carry down . . . a present . . . a little honey." Genesis 43:11

13 −5	13 −8	13 −5	13 −5	8 +5	13 −5	13 −8	5 +8
8 +5	13 −8	5 +8	8 +5	13 −5	5 +8	13 −8	13 −5
13 −8	13 −5	8 +5	13 −8	5 +8	8 +5	13 −5	5 +8
8 +5	5 +8	13 −8	8 +5	13 −5	13 −8	5 +8	13 −5
13 −8	13 −8	13 −5	13 −8	8 +5	13 −5	13 −8	5 +8

8 +5	13 −5	5 +8	13 −5	8 +5	13 −8

```
  76      97      86      35      36      84
 +45     +42     +36     +96     +93     +48
_____   _____   _____   _____   _____   _____

  53      37      89      86      55      94
 +76     +94     +32     +46     +67     +45
_____   _____   _____   _____   _____   _____

  43      33      87      57      35      93
 +96     +88     +44     +65     +97     +36
_____   _____   _____   _____   _____   _____
```

Write **S** in each **square**.

Write **T** in each **triangle**.

Write **R** in each **rectangle**.

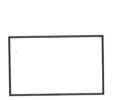

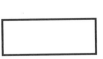

Speed Drill

13 −5	5 +8	13 −8	13 −5	8 +5	8 +5

13 −8	13 −5	13 −8	8 +5	13 −5	5 +8

5 +8	13 −5	8 +5	5 +8	13 −5	13 −8	8 +5	13 −5

13 −5	5 +8	8 +5	13 −5	5 +8	13 −8	13 −5	13 −8

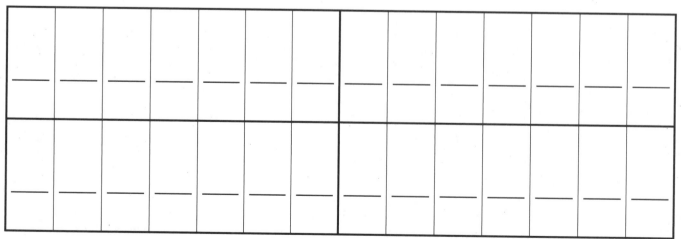

"Whatsoever thy hand findeth to do, do it with thy might." Ecclesiastes 9:10

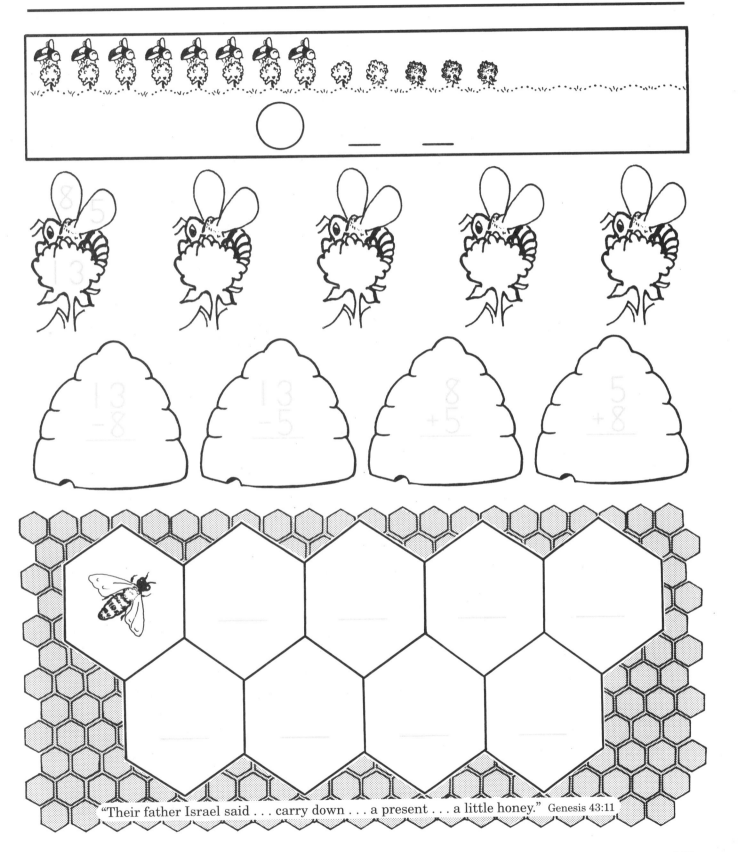

"Their father Israel said . . . carry down . . . a present . . . a little honey." Genesis 43:11

136 −86	38 +45	137 −55	136 −84	56 +83	138 −56
35 +68	139 −86	75 +55	139 −54	38 +25	139 −81
55 +28	138 −88	134 −82	135 −53	139 −57	84 +55
138 −85	58 +45	137 −52	46 +84	138 −80	35 +28
138 −83	82 +52	138 −54	78 +25	74 +56	139 −88

85 +18	137 −53	51 +83	137 −82

13 cars were stuck in snow-drifts. Father pulled 8 cars out with his truck. How many cars were still stuck in drifts?

Joy sang eight songs as she swept snow from the porch and 5 songs as she helped make pies. How many songs was that altogether?

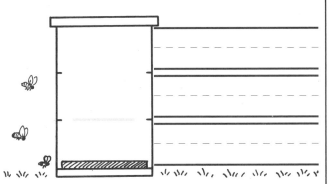

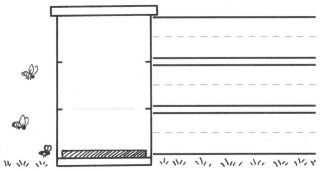

"His eye
seeth every
precious thing."

Job 28:10

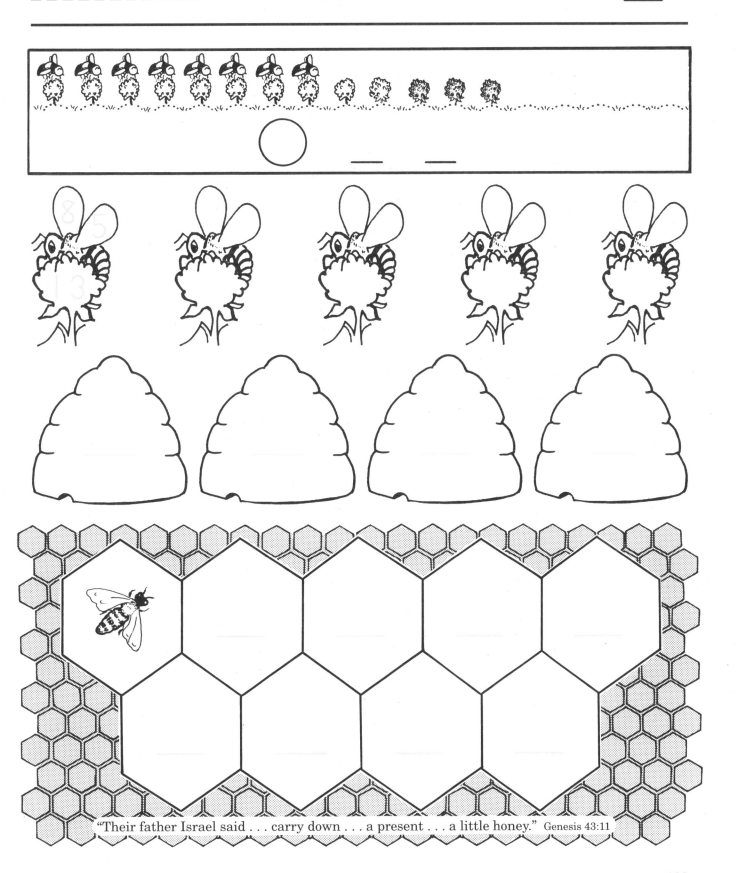

"Their father Israel said . . . carry down . . . a present . . . a little honey." Genesis 43:11

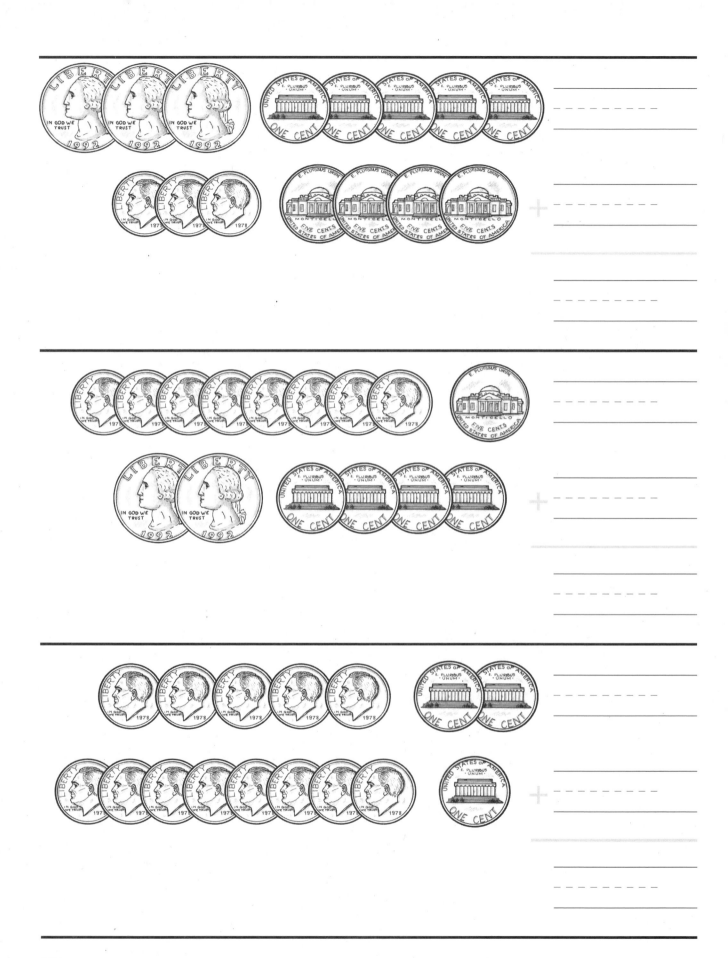

↓   ↓   ↓   ↓   ↓   ↓

93	52	81	52	71	93
-65	-16	-32	-28	-46	-49

↓   ↓   ↓   ↓   ↓   ↓

83	91	73	83	61	93
-49	-66	-49	-34	-15	-65

8	12	13	7	12	4	13	12
+5	-7	-9	+5	-6	+9	-8	-5

13	6	13	5	13	8	5	13
-5	+6	-4	+7	-5	+5	+8	-4

12	13	5	12	5	13	12	9
-5	-8	+8	-6	+7	-9	-7	+4

125

13	8	13	13	9	13
−5	+5	−8	−4	+4	−9

13	13	8	4	5	13
−8	−4	+5	+9	+8	−5

4	13	13	9	13	13	5	13
+9	−5	−9	+4	−4	−8	+8	−5

13	9	13	5	8	4	13	13
−5	+4	−5	+8	+5	+9	−4	−8

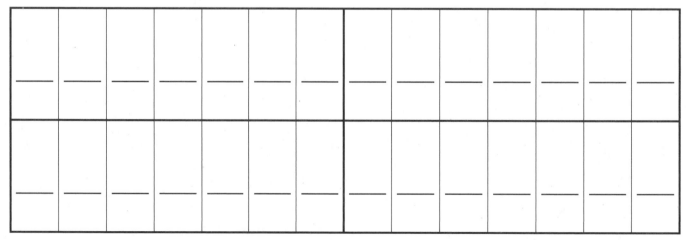

"Whatsoever thy hand findeth to do, do it with thy might." Ecclesiastes 9:10

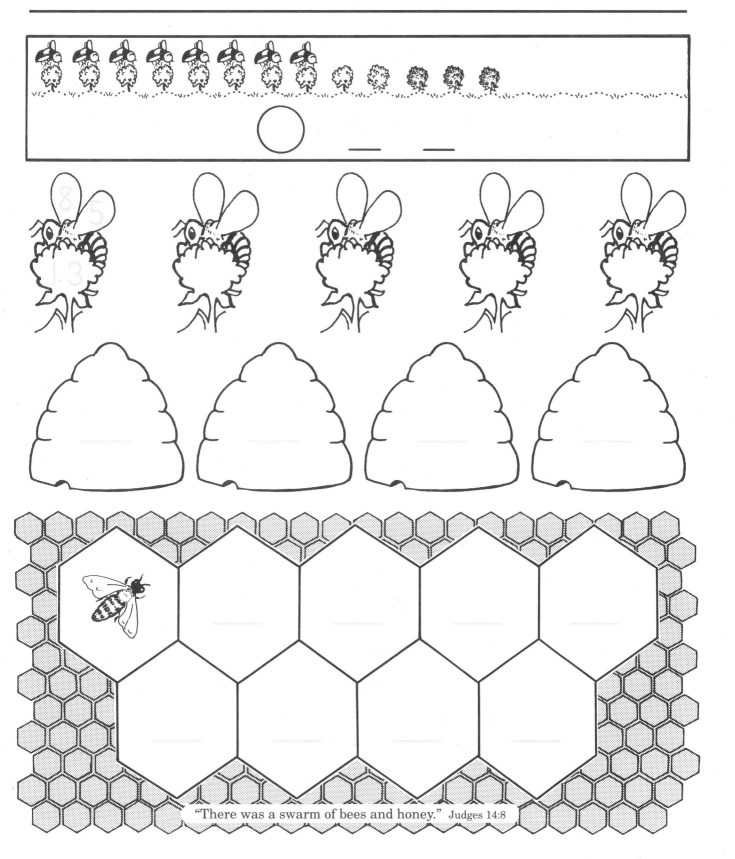

"There was a swarm of bees and honey." Judges 14:8

13 - 8 = ___	13 - ___ = 8	___ + 5 = 13
13 - 5 = ___	___ + 5 = 13	___ + 8 = 13
5 + ___ = 13	5 + 8 = ___	13 - ___ = 5
___ - 8 = 5	13 - ___ = 8	___ - 5 = 8
8 + ___ = 13	___ + 5 = 13	5 + 8 = ___
13 - ___ = 5	5 + 8 = ___	13 - ___ = 5

$$\begin{array}{cc} 4 \\ 4 \\ +5 \\ \hline \end{array} \qquad \begin{array}{cc} 3 \\ 5 \\ +3 \\ \hline \end{array} \qquad \begin{array}{cc} 3 \\ 2 \\ +8 \\ \hline \end{array} \qquad \begin{array}{cc} 3 \\ 5 \\ +5 \\ \hline \end{array} \qquad \begin{array}{cc} 5 \\ 3 \\ +2 \\ \hline \end{array} \qquad \begin{array}{cc} 1 \\ 7 \\ +5 \\ \hline \end{array} \qquad \begin{array}{cc} 1 \\ 4 \\ +8 \\ \hline \end{array} \qquad \begin{array}{cc} 2 \\ 7 \\ +3 \\ \hline \end{array}$$

$$\begin{array}{cc} 3 \\ 4 \\ +5 \\ \hline \end{array} \qquad \begin{array}{cc} 2 \\ 3 \\ +8 \\ \hline \end{array} \qquad \begin{array}{cc} 5 \\ 3 \\ +5 \\ \hline \end{array} \qquad \begin{array}{cc} 1 \\ 6 \\ +3 \\ \hline \end{array} \qquad \begin{array}{cc} 2 \\ 6 \\ +5 \\ \hline \end{array} \qquad \begin{array}{cc} 7 \\ 1 \\ +5 \\ \hline \end{array} \qquad \begin{array}{cc} 2 \\ 6 \\ +3 \\ \hline \end{array} \qquad \begin{array}{cc} 6 \\ 2 \\ +5 \\ \hline \end{array}$$

```
  ↓
 8 1        7 2        7 2        7 2        9 1        9 2
-6 9       -4 5       -2 9       -4 8       -3 6       -4 8
_____     _____     _____     _____     _____     _____
```

```
  ↓          ↓          ↓          ↓          ↓          ↓
 5 3        9 1        4 3        8 2        6 1        9 1
-2 9       -7 6       -1 9       -3 9       -1 4       -3 9
_____     _____     _____     _____     _____     _____
```

Count by
10's

100			

"His eye
seeth every
precious thing."

Job 28:10

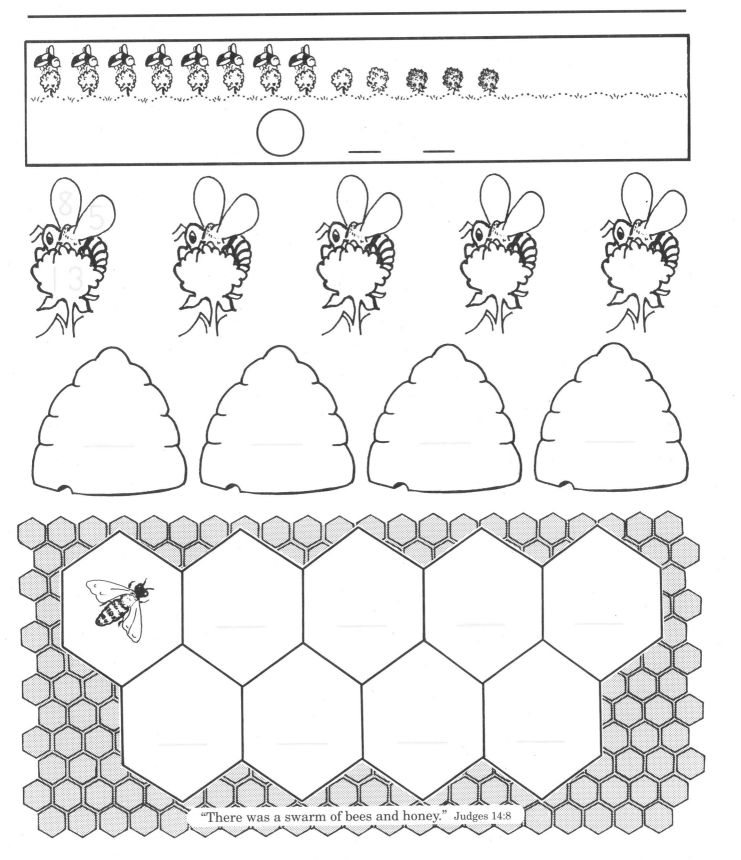

"There was a swarm of bees and honey." Judges 14:8

God sends snow. It does what I cannot do. It stops 5 cars going down a hill and 8 cars going up. How many cars is that altogether?

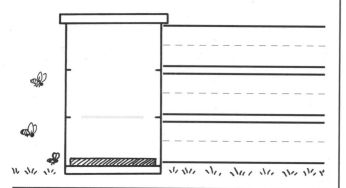

Ruth and Rose helped mend socks. Ruth mended 8 socks. Rose mended five. How many socks did both girls mend?

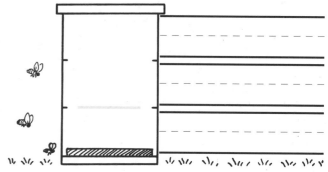

13 snow-men stand on a hill. The hot sun melts eight of them. How many snow-men stand on the hill now?

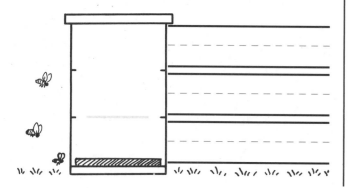

13 children sit in desks. Then five children get up and go to class. How many children are left sitting in desks?

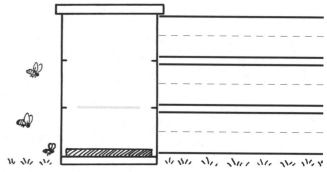

↓ 72
-48

↓ 82
-69

↓ 83
-34

↓ 73
-49

↓ 71
-46

↓ 83
-59

↓ 73
-59

↓ 51
-26

↓ 52
-28

↓ 81
-32

↓ 52
-29

↓ 93
-69

Count by **10's**

100			

133

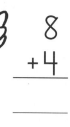

13	13	5	12	8	13
-5	-8	+8	-8	+4	-5

8	5	12	4	12	13
+4	+8	-4	+8	-8	-8

12	5	13	4	12	8	13	13
-4	+8	-5	+8	-8	+5	-8	-5

8	13	13	12	8	12	5	4
+5	-5	-8	-8	+4	-4	+8	+8

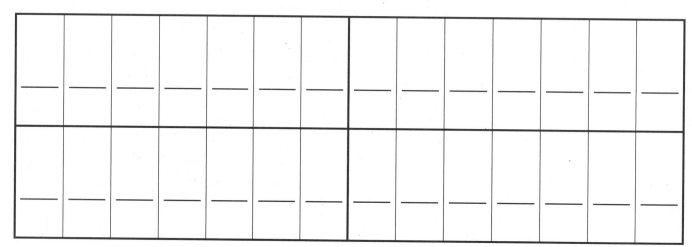

"Whatsoever thy hand findeth to do, do it with thy might." Ecclesiastes 9:10

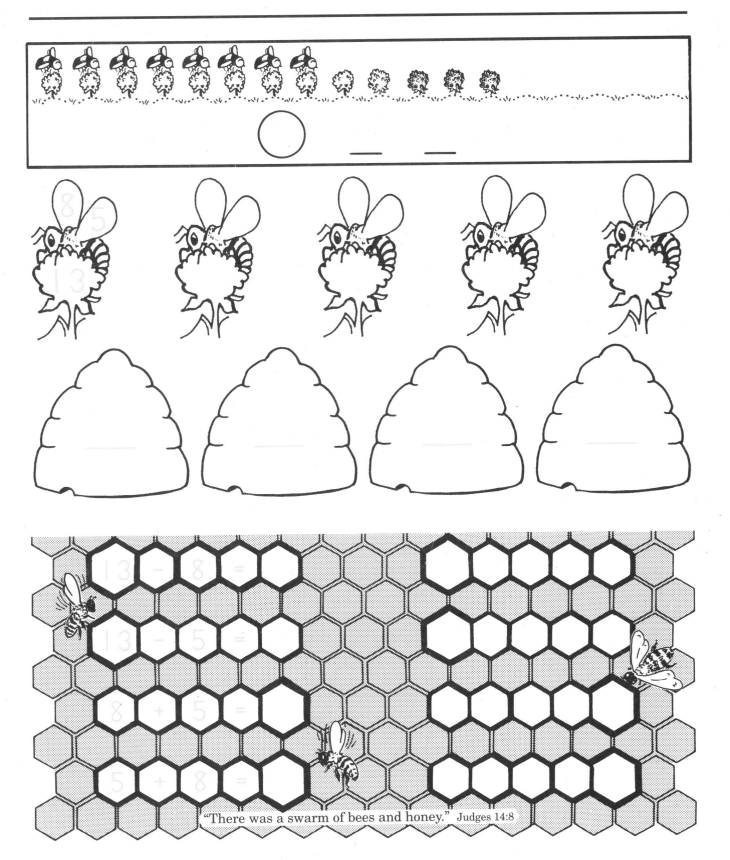

"There was a swarm of bees and honey." Judges 14:8

13	12	13	13	8	13	12	8
−8	−4	−8	−5	+4	−8	−4	+5

5	12	8	4	13	5	12	13
+8	−8	+5	+8	−5	+8	−8	−8

13	12	8	12	4	5	12	4
−5	−8	+5	−4	+8	+8	−8	+8

8	8	13	8	12	13	5	13
+4	+5	−8	+4	−4	−8	+8	−5

12	13	12	13	13	12	13	5
−8	−5	−4	−5	−8	−4	−5	+8

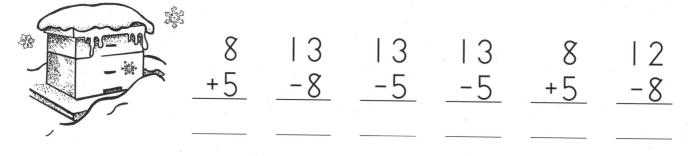

8	13	13	13	8	12
+5	−8	−5	−5	+5	−8

93 -48	77 -51	83 -39	92 -65	98 -72	89 -53
72 -36	98 -44	83 -54	71 -35	89 -35	62 -33
79 -43	67 -41	81 -54	63 -19	98 -72	83 -38

Count by **10's**

200			

"His eye
seeth every
precious thing."

Job 28:10

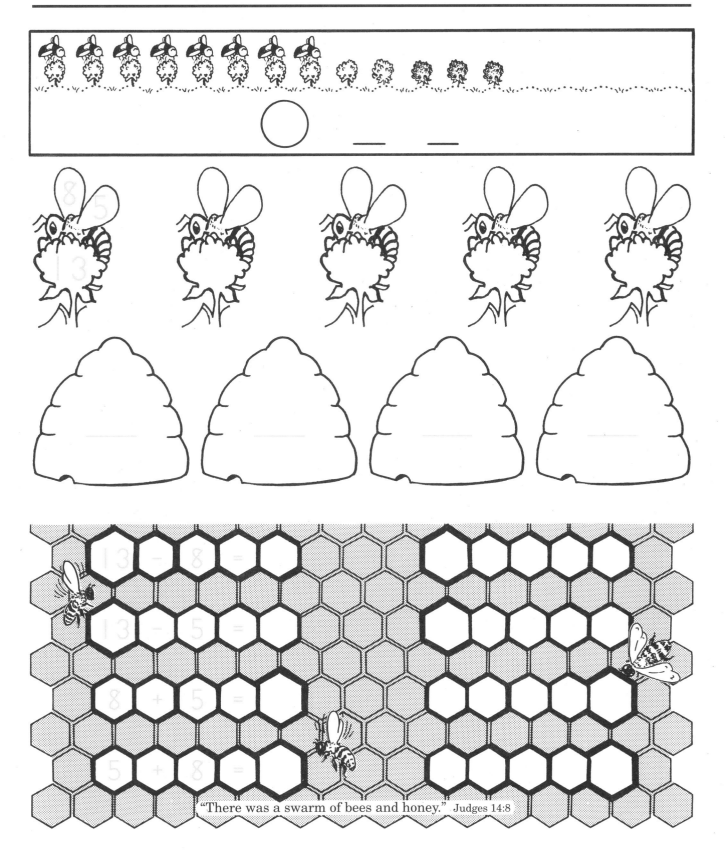

$$13 - 8 =$$

$$13 - 5 =$$

$$8 + 5 =$$

$$5 + 8 =$$

"There was a swarm of bees and honey." Judges 14:8

12	13	13	13	3	11	12	8
-8	-5	-9	-9	+9	-7	-4	+4

5	12	8	9	12	5	12	11
+8	-9	+3	+4	-8	+6	-9	-7

11	11	5	12	6	9	12	7
-5	-8	+8	-6	+6	+4	-9	+5

9	3	12	6	11	11	5	11
+2	+9	-7	+5	-9	-6	+7	-9

13	13	11	11	4	12	13	8
-5	-8	-4	-3	+9	-5	-8	+5

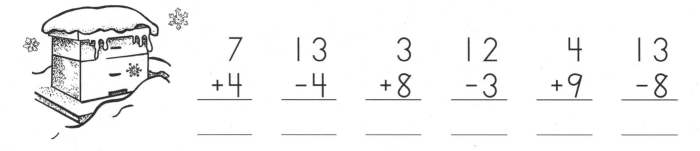

		7	13	3	12	4	13
		+4	-4	+8	-3	+9	-8

140

```
  62        72        98        83        83        98
 -33       -36       -72       -38       -39       -44
_____    _____    _____    _____    _____    _____


  67        81        79        98        89        92
 -41       -54       -43       -72       -53       -65
_____    _____    _____    _____    _____    _____


  71        83        93        77        89        63
 -35       -54       -48       -51       -35       -19
_____    _____    _____    _____    _____    _____
```

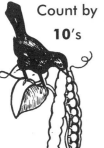

Count by 10's

200			

Speed Drill

5 +8	4 +9	5 +7	8 +5	9 +3	9 +4

8 +4	6 +6	9 +4	7 +5	8 +5	4 +9

6 +6	4 +9	9 +4	5 +7	8 +5	4 +8	9 +4	5 +8

8 +5	3 +9	5 +8	4 +9	6 +6	8 +5	7 +5	8 +4

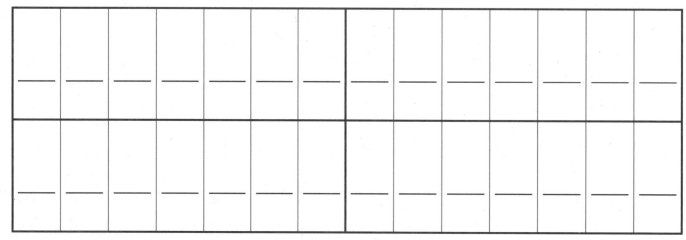

"Whatsoever thy hand findeth to do, do it with thy might." Ecclesiastes 9:10

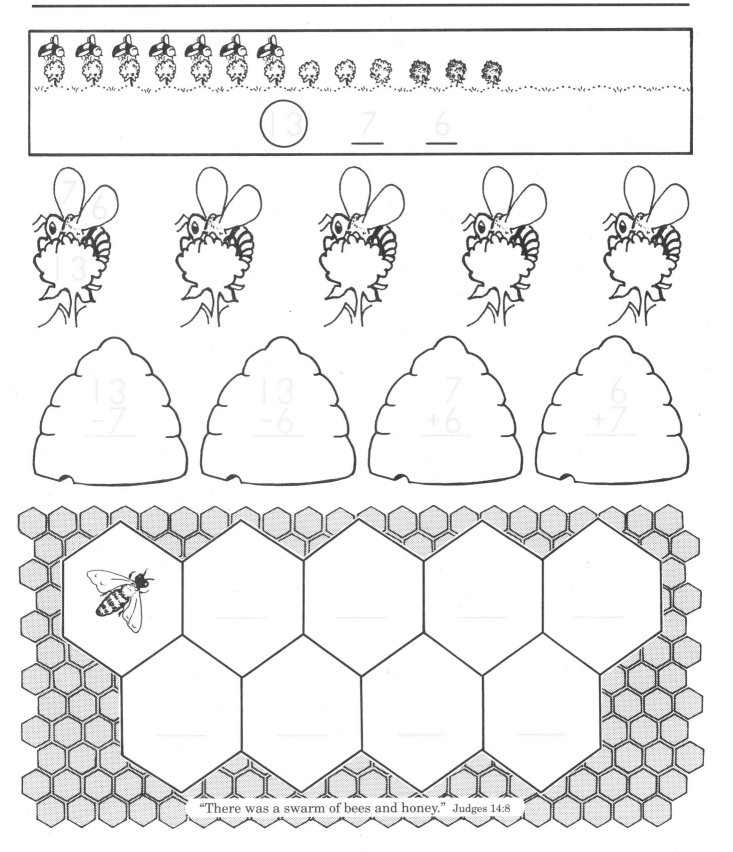

"There was a swarm of bees and honey." Judges 14:8

143

13	13	13	13	6	13	13	7
-7	-6	-7	-6	+7	-7	-6	+6

6	13	6	7	13	7	13	13
+7	-6	+7	+6	-6	+6	-6	-7

13	13	6	13	7	6	13	6
-6	-7	+7	-7	+6	+7	-7	+7

7	6	13	6	13	13	7	13
+6	+7	-6	+7	-7	-6	+6	-6

13	13	13	13	13	13	13	7
-7	-6	-7	-6	-7	-7	-6	+6

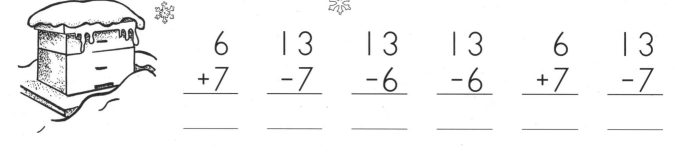

	6	13	13	13	6	13
	+7	-7	-6	-6	+7	-7

93	69	93	99	83	83
-25	-57	-69	-65	-64	-38

82	67	92	68	98	92
-46	-24	-57	-32	-63	-49

91	92	68	82	58	82
-46	-73	-34	-58	-46	-14

"His eye seeth every precious thing."

Job 28:10

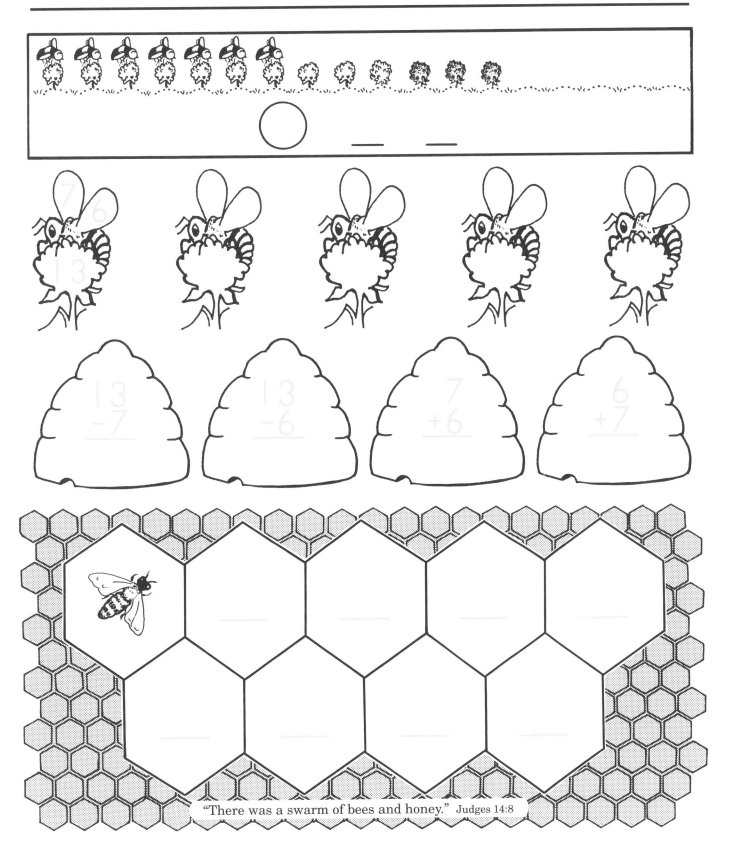

$$\bigcirc \quad \underline{} \quad \underline{} \quad \underline{}$$

$$\begin{array}{r} 13 \\ -7 \\ \hline \end{array} \qquad \begin{array}{r} 13 \\ -6 \\ \hline \end{array} \qquad \begin{array}{r} 7 \\ +6 \\ \hline \end{array} \qquad \begin{array}{r} 6 \\ +7 \\ \hline \end{array}$$

"There was a swarm of bees and honey." Judges 14:8

13	13	13	13	6	13	13	7
-6	-7	-6	-6	+7	-6	-7	+6

7	13	6	7	13	6	13	13
+6	-6	+7	+6	-6	+7	-6	-6

13	13	6	13	7	6	13	6
-7	-7	+7	-6	+6	+7	-7	+7

7	6	13	6	13	13	7	13
+6	+7	-6	+7	-6	-6	+6	-7

13	13	13	13	13	13	13	7
-6	-6	-7	-6	-7	-7	-6	+6

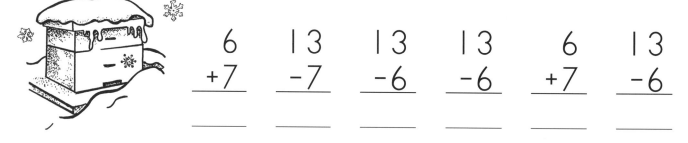

6	13	13	13	6	13
+7	-7	-6	-6	+7	-6

```
  66        52        33        44        23        55
  23        37        41        22        66        40
 +44       +23       +52       +53       +44       +41
 ____      ____      ____      ____      ____      ____
```

```
  15        60        22        46        43        47
  23        34        73        22        30        41
 +94       +42       +24       +55       +43       +45
 ____      ____      ____      ____      ____      ____
```

Fay and Mae scrub and scrub. Fay scrubs seven windows. Mae scrubs six windows. How many windows do both girls scrub?

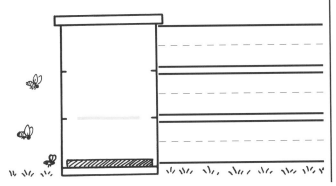

Carl has twelve rabbits in a pen. 7 rabbits hop out of the pen. How many rabbits are left in the pen?

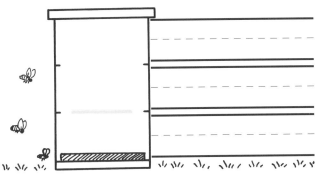

Speed
Drill

13 -6	7 +6	6 +7	13 -7	7 +6	13 -6

13 -7	13 -6	6 +7	13 -6	7 +6	6 +7

13 -7	6 +7	13 -6	7 +6	13 -7	6 +7	7 +6	13 -6

6 +7	13 -7	7 +6	6 +7	13 -6	7 +6	13 -6	13 -7

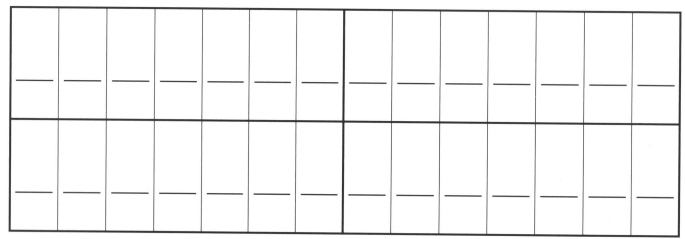

"Whatsoever thy hand findeth to do, do it with thy might." Ecclesiastes 9:10

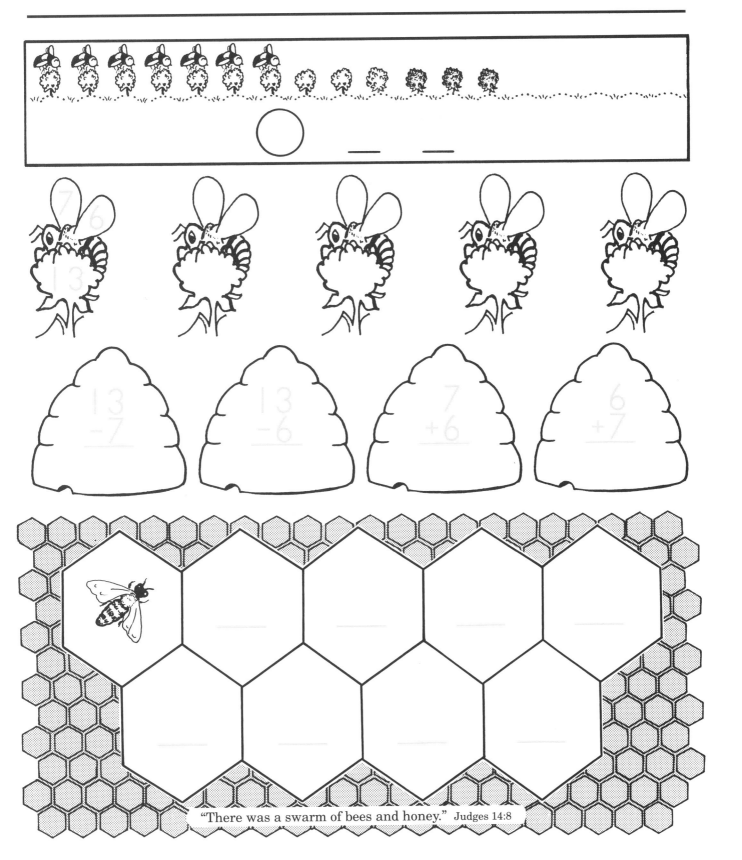

○ ___ ___

| 13 | 13 | 7 | 6 |
| −7 | −6 | +6 | +7 |

"There was a swarm of bees and honey." Judges 14:8

139 −72	37 +46	137 −65	136 −74	66 +73	138 −66
37 +66	139 −76	65 +72	139 −64	36 +27	133 −63
46 +37	138 −71	134 −72	135 −63	139 −67	74 +65
138 −75	56 +47	135 −60	73 +64	137 −67	37 +26
138 −73	76 +17	138 −64	73 +65	26 +77	139 −78

64 +74	137 −63	27 +66	137 −72

	thousands	hundreds	tens	ones
1784	___ ,	___	___	___
815	___ ,	___	___	___
1945	___ ,	___	___	___
16	___ ,	___	___	___
1325	___ ,	___	___	___
1784	___ ,	___	___	___
1406	___ ,	___	___	___

	thousands	hundreds	tens	ones
784	___ ,	___	___	___
1623	___ ,	___	___	___
80	___ ,	___	___	___
1315	___ ,	___	___	___
293	___ ,	___	___	___
1324	___ ,	___	___	___
1583	___ ,	___	___	___

_____   _____   _____   _____   _____

_____   _____   _____   _____   _____

"His eye
seeth every
precious thing."

Job 28:10

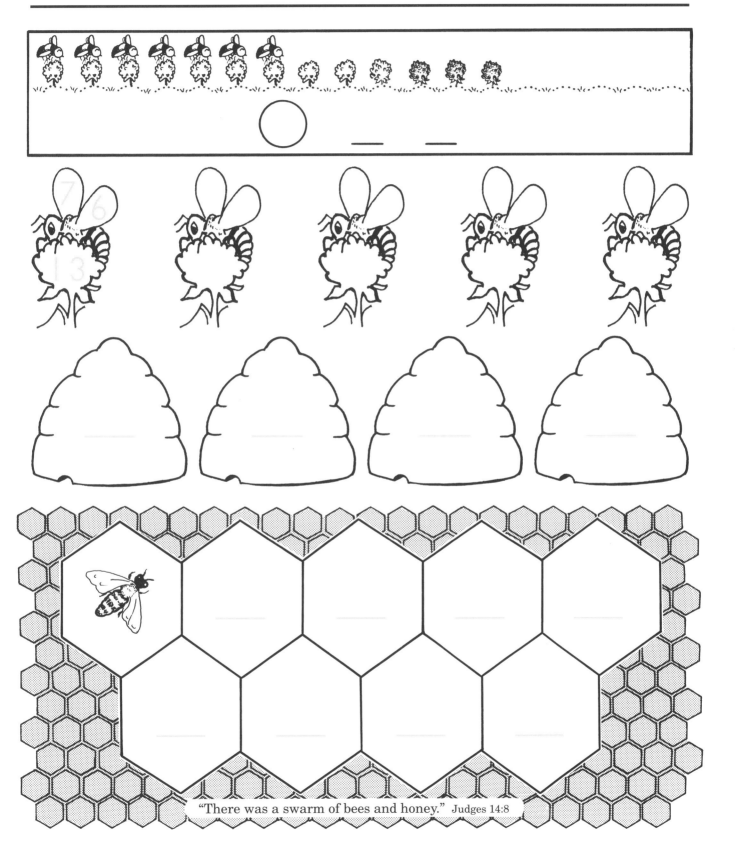

"There was a swarm of bees and honey." Judges 14:8

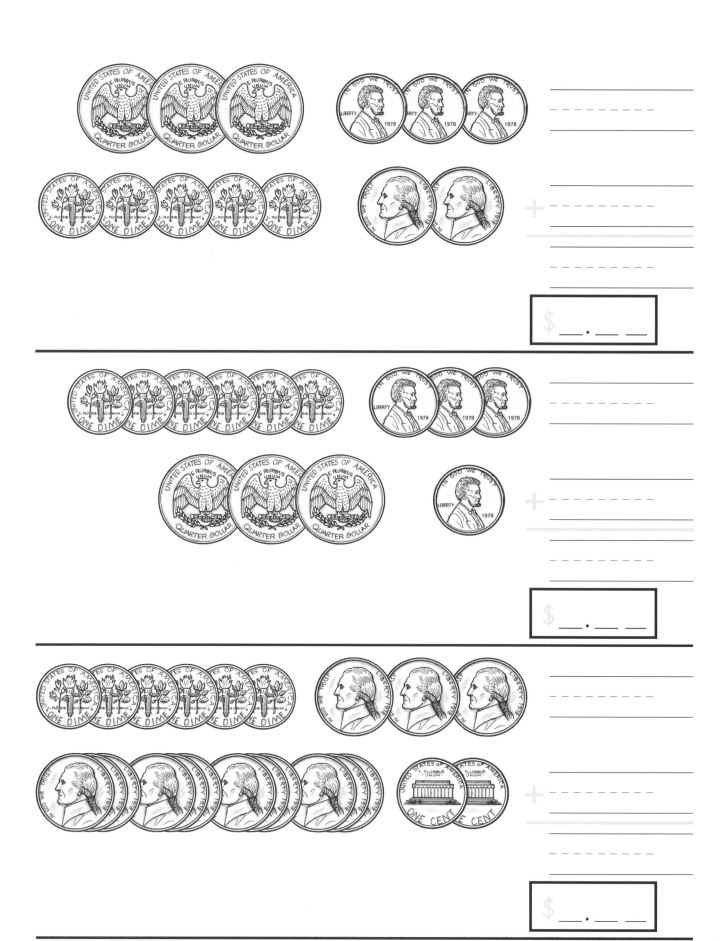

63	35	42	33	33	59
- 5	- 1	- 8	- 8	- 9	- 3

72	98	83	73	89	63
-36	-44	-58	-39	-35	-35

13	13	12	13	9	13	13	8
-9	-5	-7	-9	+4	-8	-5	+5

7	13	4	5	13	8	13	12
+5	-7	+9	+7	-8	+5	-7	-7

13	12	5	13	6	7	13	5
-4	-5	+7	-4	+7	+5	-6	+8

6	7	13	5	13	12	5	13
+7	+5	-8	+8	-5	-7	+7	-5

**Speed
Drill**

7 +6	6 +7	13 −6	8 +5	13 −5	13 −7
___	___	___	___	___	___

13 −8	13 −5	13 −7	7 +6	5 +8	13 −6
___	___	___	___	___	___

13 −8	5 +8	13 −7	13 −5	8 +5	13 −6	7 +6	8 +5
___	___	___	___	___	___	___	___

6 +7	13 −8	13 −6	6 +7	5 +8	13 −7	13 −5	13 −8
___	___	___	___	___	___	___	___

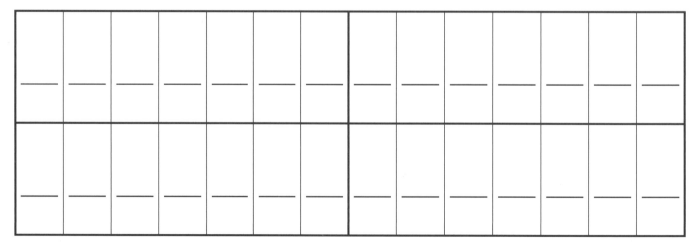

"Whatsoever thy hand findeth to do, do it with thy might." Ecclesiastes 9:10

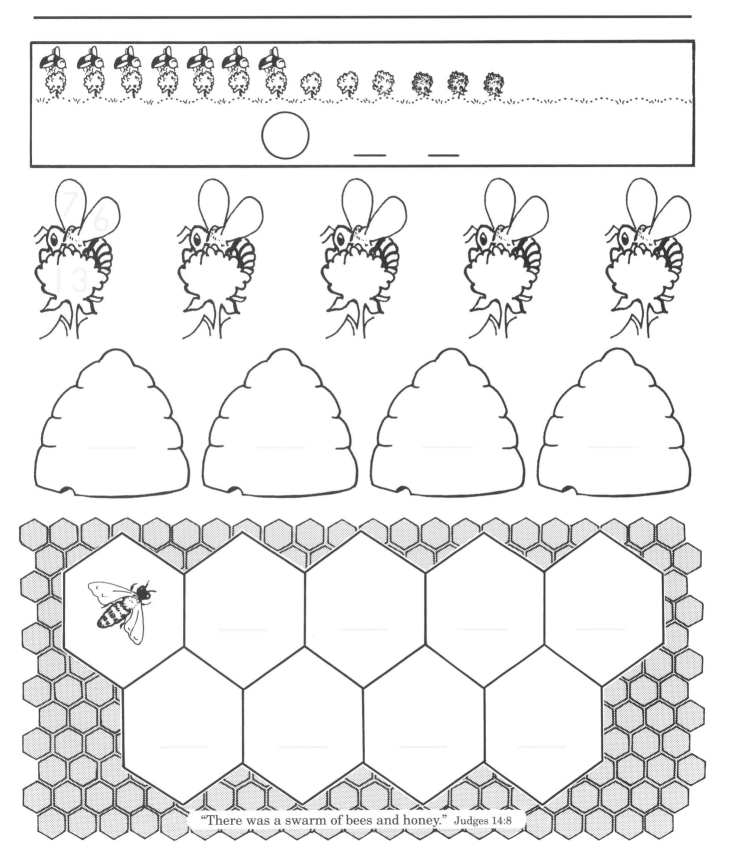

"There was a swarm of bees and honey." Judges 14:8

6 + 7 = ___	13 - ___ = 6	6 + 7 = ___
13 - 7 = ___	13 - 6 = ___	13 - 7 = ___
13 - ___ = 7	7 + 6 = ___	___ - 6 = 7
___ + 6 = 13	6 + ___ = 13	7 + 6 = ___
13 - ___ = 7	___ + 7 = 13	6 + ___ = 13
___ + 6 = 13	13 - ___ = 6	___ - 7 = 6

$$\begin{array}{r} 4 \\ 2 \\ +7 \\ \hline \end{array} \qquad \begin{array}{r} 3 \\ 2 \\ +5 \\ \hline \end{array} \qquad \begin{array}{r} 4 \\ 3 \\ +4 \\ \hline \end{array} \qquad \begin{array}{r} 3 \\ 3 \\ +7 \\ \hline \end{array} \qquad \begin{array}{r} 2 \\ 5 \\ +6 \\ \hline \end{array} \qquad \begin{array}{r} 5 \\ 2 \\ +6 \\ \hline \end{array} \qquad \begin{array}{r} 2 \\ 6 \\ +4 \\ \hline \end{array} \qquad \begin{array}{r} 8 \\ 1 \\ +4 \\ \hline \end{array}$$

$$\begin{array}{r} 5 \\ 4 \\ +4 \\ \hline \end{array} \qquad \begin{array}{r} 2 \\ 4 \\ +6 \\ \hline \end{array} \qquad \begin{array}{r} 1 \\ 5 \\ +7 \\ \hline \end{array} \qquad \begin{array}{r} 6 \\ 1 \\ +6 \\ \hline \end{array} \qquad \begin{array}{r} 4 \\ 3 \\ +6 \\ \hline \end{array} \qquad \begin{array}{r} 3 \\ 1 \\ +7 \\ \hline \end{array} \qquad \begin{array}{r} 4 \\ 2 \\ +4 \\ \hline \end{array} \qquad \begin{array}{r} 2 \\ 5 \\ +6 \\ \hline \end{array}$$

```
  93      72      93      89      93      89
 -37     -35     -68     -17     -76     -58
_____   _____   _____   _____   _____   _____
```

```
  88      81      98      82      93      82
 -57     -24     -26     -57     -56     -66
_____   _____   _____   _____   _____   _____
```

Count by **2's**

200			

"His eye
seeth every
precious thing."

Job 28:10

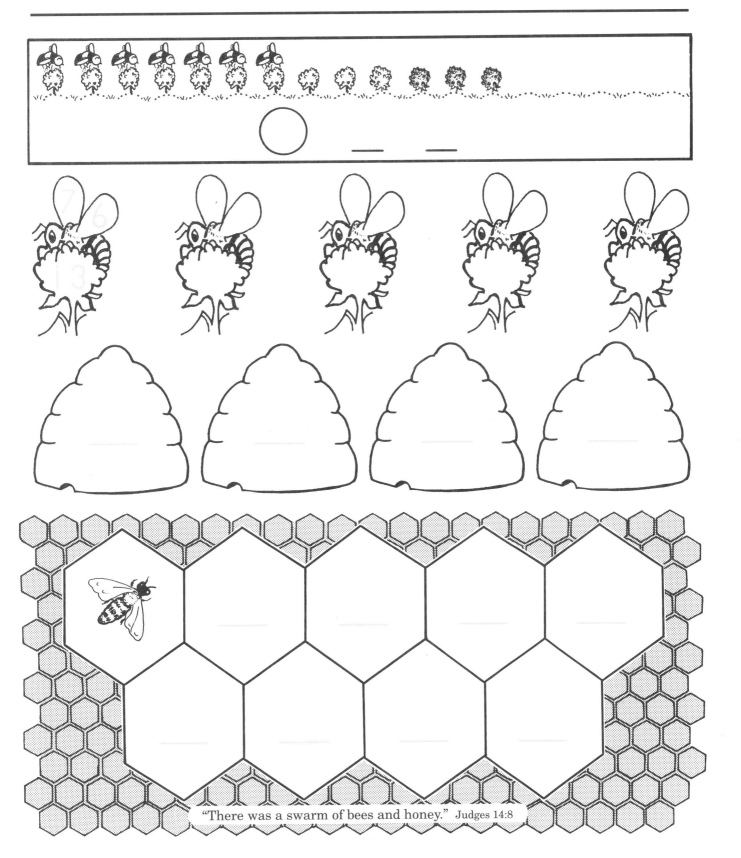

"There was a swarm of bees and honey." Judges 14:8

Fred found 13 eggs in the hen house. Six eggs were brown. The rest were white. How many eggs were white?

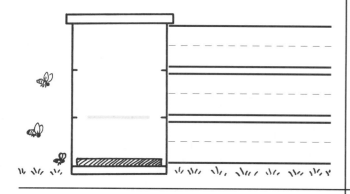

Glen and Fay helped Mother clean the church. Glen dusted 7 benches. Fay dusted six. How many benches did both children dust?

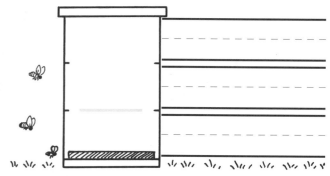

Mother hung twelve mittens on the line to dry. 8 mittens were blue. The rest were green. How many mittens were green?

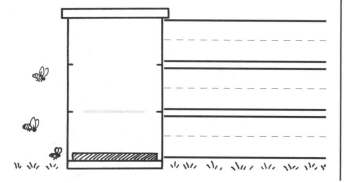

Thirteen fish swim in a bowl. Seven fish are small. The rest are big. How many fish are big?

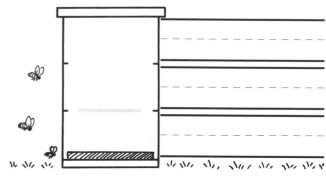

```
  77        86        44        88        94        66
 +56       +36       +27       +50       +45       +72
_____    _____    _____    _____    _____    _____


  76        65        65        62        79        87
 +57       +70       +48       +53       +54       +46
_____    _____    _____    _____    _____    _____


  77        88        53        33        54        63
 +45       +45       +85       +38       +84       +76
_____    _____    _____    _____    _____    _____
```

Write $\frac{1}{2}$ on each **half**.

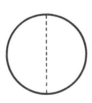
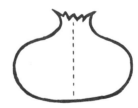
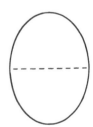

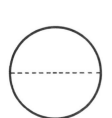

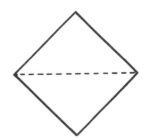
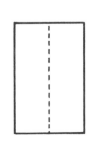

165

Speed Drill

5	13	7	12	12	13
+7	−6	+6	−7	−5	−7

6	13	12	7	7	12
+7	−7	−5	+6	+5	−7

13	5	13	12	12	6	13	5
−6	+7	−7	−5	−7	+7	−6	+7

7	12	12	5	6	13	13	7
+5	−5	−7	+7	+7	−6	−7	+6

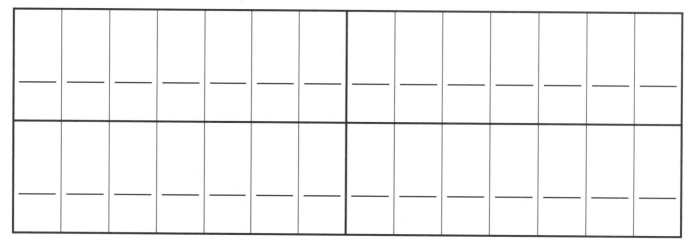

"Whatsoever thy hand findeth to do, do it with thy might." Ecclesiastes 9:10

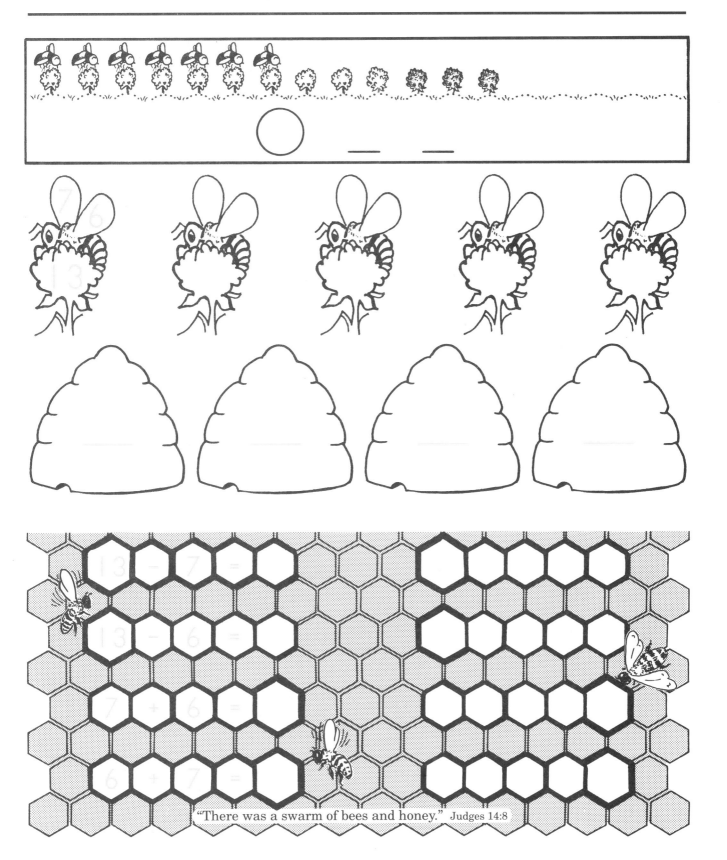

"There was a swarm of bees and honey." Judges 14:8

167

13	13	12	13	6	12	13	7
-7	-6	-5	-6	+7	-5	-6	+6

6	13	5	7	13	7	13	13
+7	-6	+7	+6	-6	+5	-6	-7

12	13	6	13	5	6	13	6
-7	-7	+7	-7	+7	+7	-7	+7

7	6	13	7	13	13	7	12
+6	+7	-6	+5	-7	-6	+6	-7

7	13	12	13	13	12	12	7
+5	-6	-7	-6	-7	-7	-5	+6

6	13	13	12	6	5
+7	-7	-6	-5	+7	+7

168

```
  73        98        93        82        99        93
 -46       -75       -37       -55       -74       -35
_____     _____     _____     _____     _____     _____


  93        93        92        82        99        98
 -48       -14       -57       -43       -23       -52
_____     _____     _____     _____     _____     _____


  72        87        73        83        68        82
 -14       -62       -46       -27       -45       -55
_____     _____     _____     _____     _____     _____
```

Write ½ on each **half**.

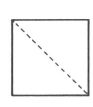 

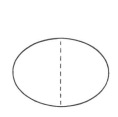  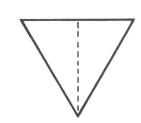 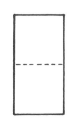 

"His eye
seeth every
precious thing."

Job 28:10

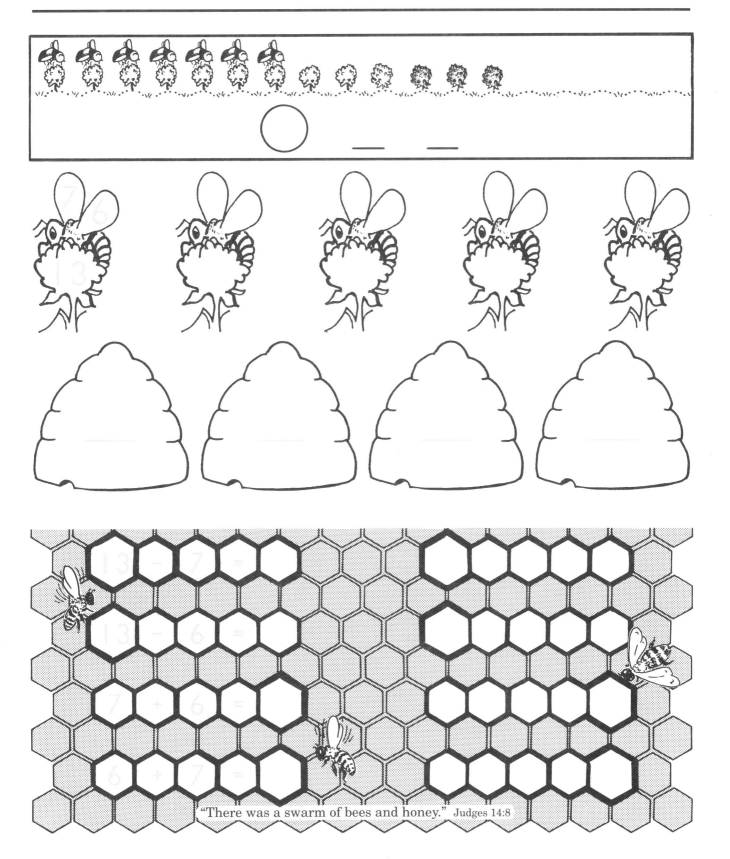

"There was a swarm of bees and honey." Judges 14:8

13	11	13	11	6	12	12	3
-7	-7	-8	-2	+7	-7	-8	+9

4	12	3	7	13	2	13	11
+8	-5	+8	+6	-4	+9	-6	-5

13	13	6	13	5	4	12	6
-5	-7	+7	-9	+8	+9	-6	+6

5	6	13	9	12	12	7	11
+7	+7	-4	+4	-8	-3	+6	-3

13	13	12	11	12	11	13	7
-5	-6	-9	-9	-7	-8	-6	+6

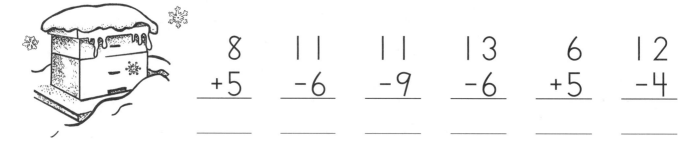

8	11	11	13	6	12
+5	-6	-9	-6	+5	-4

| 139
-76 | 36
+57 | 139
-64 | 118
-47 | 35
+17 | 137
-94 |

| 88
+45 | 128
-48 | 46
+77 | 118
-36 | 53
+85 | 139
-77 |

| 26
+17 | 135
-83 | 139
-68 | 127
-52 | 138
-45 | 28
+35 |

Write ½ on each **half**.

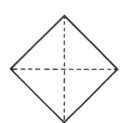
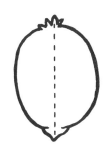

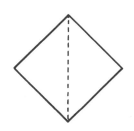
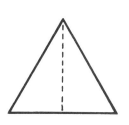

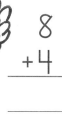

**Speed
Drill**

$$\begin{array}{r} 4 \\ +8 \\ \hline \end{array} \quad \begin{array}{r} 9 \\ +4 \\ \hline \end{array} \quad \begin{array}{r} 9 \\ +3 \\ \hline \end{array} \quad \begin{array}{r} 7 \\ +5 \\ \hline \end{array} \quad \begin{array}{r} 8 \\ +5 \\ \hline \end{array} \quad \begin{array}{r} 6 \\ +6 \\ \hline \end{array}$$

$$\begin{array}{r} 8 \\ +4 \\ \hline \end{array} \quad \begin{array}{r} 7 \\ +6 \\ \hline \end{array} \quad \begin{array}{r} 5 \\ +8 \\ \hline \end{array} \quad \begin{array}{r} 9 \\ +4 \\ \hline \end{array} \quad \begin{array}{r} 5 \\ +7 \\ \hline \end{array} \quad \begin{array}{r} 6 \\ +7 \\ \hline \end{array}$$

$$\begin{array}{r} 6 \\ +7 \\ \hline \end{array} \quad \begin{array}{r} 4 \\ +9 \\ \hline \end{array} \quad \begin{array}{r} 7 \\ +5 \\ \hline \end{array} \quad \begin{array}{r} 7 \\ +6 \\ \hline \end{array} \quad \begin{array}{r} 3 \\ +9 \\ \hline \end{array} \quad \begin{array}{r} 6 \\ +6 \\ \hline \end{array} \quad \begin{array}{r} 8 \\ +5 \\ \hline \end{array} \quad \begin{array}{r} 8 \\ +4 \\ \hline \end{array}$$

$$\begin{array}{r} 3 \\ 4 \\ +6 \\ \hline \end{array} \quad \begin{array}{r} 2 \\ 3 \\ +8 \\ \hline \end{array} \quad \begin{array}{r} 3 \\ 3 \\ +7 \\ \hline \end{array} \quad \begin{array}{r} 5 \\ 2 \\ +5 \\ \hline \end{array} \quad \begin{array}{r} 4 \\ 4 \\ +5 \\ \hline \end{array} \quad \begin{array}{r} 2 \\ 6 \\ +5 \\ \hline \end{array} \quad \begin{array}{r} 3 \\ 1 \\ +9 \\ \hline \end{array} \quad \begin{array}{r} 3 \\ 5 \\ +4 \\ \hline \end{array}$$

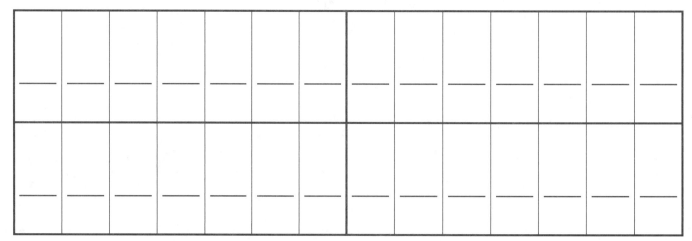

"Whatsoever thy hand findeth to do, do it with thy might." Ecclesiastes 9:10